To my dear friend Ru
Thanks for you
for over 25 years
Love [signature]

Dear Sis

The Abuse is Over!

By

Vawn Gretta

Dear Sis, The Abuse is Over!

Written by Vawn Gretta

Graphics and Design by Christ-Like Graphics

Copyright © 2016 by Wisdom Entertainment

All rights reserved. No part of this book may be reproduced or transmitted in any form or by any means without written permission of the author.

For order information and booking please visit:

www.vawngretta.com

Visit on Facebook:

Vawn Gretta and Wisdom Entertainment

Acknowledgments

For my family, I thank God totally for you. I love my children for sharing me with my purpose. This is a ministry book. I am serving and glorifying God so brace yourselves. God told me what to write and that I must be completely honest and real even in the areas where it is difficult. I love and cherish my parents for all they have poured into me. I adore my mother, for being so strong; for, it is truly her silent strength that showed me how to never give up and continue the fight. There is absolutely no way I could have made it this far without you and God knows it. I thank God for my sisters in Christ, Koby Mitchell, Linda Van de Byl, Doranna Longino and Andrea Midget. You teach me way more than you know, believe that! For my personal cheerleader and baby sis, Nechelle Myers, I just love you. I want to give God the total glory for Pastors, Jerome and Betty Nelson, Sr. of Spirit of Life Ministries, for just everything. I want to give God maximum glory for Joel Osteen for loving me out of the darkness, to the light through the encouragement of God's love for me. It is way too hard to sum it up in this book all that you all have poured of yourself into my life.

To my children Bunny, Bear and Kitty – you all are my truest besties. Oh, I love you so much. Love you all.

Foreword

My sisters this is going to be an exciting journey both for you and me. First let me say that the point of this book is to not just share all of my business as if it is a soap opera, but to give a clear picture of what I went through and what I learned as a result. This is truly a journey from darkness to light. So please know that there will be graphic details. The only way I can minister and share is from a state of pure truth. Inside of that truth lies the true picture of a misguided life (self-induced at the time) to a directional life in the salvation process. Because of this honesty, my hope and prayer is that my sisters will see possible traps before them and not get ensnared; and, if you have already been caught up, you will have to courage to walk away from a detrimental situation. I wrote this book from a conservation perspective. I wanted this to be as if we were having a girlfriend talk so that the subject matter will be more approachable.

The purpose of this book is to know we are not alone and that we are abundantly loved. Loved so much that we can go through life no matter how hard or how wonderful and still have joy no matter what happens. Also, God can mold us into a woman of God. You will see the depth of misunderstanding I had about what a "good man" is and if there are any left in the world. We will discover ultimately what it took to reach a peace in being unmarried and finally waiting for my husband to find me if that was in God's will for my life. My prayer is that you will have the boldness to go before God to discover if matrimony is for you meaning if that is His plan for your life. I had to get before God and ask Him that and trust me it wasn't easy. What if He said no? Does that mean that living a life without a man means it is insignificant to live my life with me and Jesus alone? It means we trust God.

God will allow through these pages a testimony of a journey that will allow us to see how we can get trapped in an untrue sense of what He has for our lives and how we can get back on a plain path that He creates for us. To be honest I really didn't want to write this book for the simple reason of not wanting to revisit the past. However, I know that God allowed the incidents you are going to read about for a reason, and, the reason is ministry. A testimony backed with the power of the word of God is the best teacher. This is true for all of us. (2 Corinthians 1:1-4)That is one of the most explosive ways to communicate how to achieve and overcome in all situations. That's right – I said all. How is that possible you say? Vawn you really don't know what I have been through, you say. Well, this is what I do say and what I do know. God, the one true and living God, will bring you through anything victoriously if you let Him.

Quite frankly just beginning this book has my stomach turning in knots. It is a fact that if we have unresolved issues inside of us that we ask for a breakdown somewhere in our life. We really have to fearlessly deal with these situations so that we are not stuck in life. I know that sounds a bit difficult, yet I am asking that you trust God with that truth. The freedom you will gain will amaze and bless your life. I am crying even now because my past is a scary place. Not all of my past is, but when I came to know Jesus and experienced His love, oh Lord Jesus I realized just how lost I was in this world; and basically, why the world and the prince of the world (the devil) were able to conquer me so much. But you want to know what is so good? God loved me first so much, that even then I was still protected. *Romans 5:8 But God commendeth his love toward us, in that, while we were yet sinners, Christ died for us.* Glory to God! I am praying that I will be totally obedient and include those things that God wants even if it is difficult for me to look at again. I believe in the beginning of my true walk with Christ I gave God all of these situations and asked Him to heal my heart totally. God did that faithfully. Yet just to know I was there and that you may be there now hurts my heart. The good news is we are not the first women to go through these things and we will not be the last to come out of these awful situations with flying colors victoriously. Maybe you have never experienced harmful situations in relationships in your past or present. That's great. Misery does NOT love company over here. However, I believe there are still some key ingredients that you will be able to mix in and/ or add to your daily walk that will empower you while God molds you and gets you ready for matrimony if it is in His will for your life to do so.

My beginning encouragement is for you to begin keeping a journal. Why? The answer is because it is so important to communicate with God. It will also help you feel like you are gaining a best friend within yourself. Who better to communicate than with God and a best friend? So find your perfect pen to write with. Don't type. Write. Pour out your heart to yourself and God. Get your favorite color highlighter and mark some of the areas you read in this book that hit home in your heart. Then write in your journal why you relate. Take time to ponder the scriptures that are noted. Don't just take my word for it either. Look them up for yourself. This means you may have to invest in a bible if you don't already have one. Alrighty? So let us begin this journey by praying first.

Beginning Prayer:

Father God you are the author and finisher of all things. You are the beginning and the end and in you, we move and have our very being. We thank you, Lord, for your strength. Anoint us God with honesty so that we may be healed. Let us give you the truth through this journey so that we may draw closer to you, trust you and never let go. I pray for a secure surrounding for not only myself as I write this book, but for the many sisters that will read this book to pour out their hearts generously to you. Let a change manifest in us like never before that will cause us to walk this life you have so lovingly given us God. We want to courageously allow you to go in the areas we have run from or covered up over time. Thank you, God, for this opportunity to share with you and each other. We bless you God for loving us first. Because you allowed different people, situations, and issues to happen to us or around us, we know you will allow them not to overcome us; but, for us to stand, victoriously over all things for we know that all things work together for the good to them that love God, to them who are the called according to your purpose. And we thank you God that you have entrusted a special purpose in all of us. We praise you God and give you glory in the matchless name of your son Christ Jesus of Nazareth. Amen.

Chapter 1 – The Beginning

And now [brethren], I commit you to God [I deposit you in His charge, entrusting you to His protection and care]. And I commend you to the Word of His grace [to the commands and counsels and promises of His unmerited favor]. It is able to build you up and to give you [your rightful] inheritance among all God's set-apart ones (those consecrated, purified, and transformed of soul)." Acts 20:32

So let's start as far back as I can remember with what I know to be my first encounter with situations that just were not from God but allowed by Him. What do I mean by this? Ok, let's get this straight from the beginning. I am a teacher ok? I am going to do my best to explain some things so that you can get it in regards to God and His ways. If I don't explain something you are reading in a way that you totally understand please seek your pastor for guidance. God is not a bulldog or an ignorant tyrant. He gives us choice. He will not force anything on us. It is important to cover our children in prayer. We have to trust God in all things. There is evil present in this world. I find that people accept that fact more than they accept that God is full of love and kindness. An interesting thought isn't it?

I am going to take you back to my 3rd-grade year. One of my classmates decided she would tell me her 4th-grade cousin Rob wanted to be my boyfriend. I met him at recess or something and decided we would play later because he lived close to me. Catch that because we have to be careful about what is close to our babies and be real with them so they don't get caught up in ignorance. Anyway, child, I was still playing with dolls. I decided I really didn't want a boyfriend because I'd rather play with my dolls and listen to my Candy Girl album! (Yeah, we are going to laugh a little too.) Now, remember this about Rob while I take you through that summer after we met.

I was at my girlfriend's house down the street from my house. I just loved getting out of my house away from my brother. Her grandmother was usually home and her mother was gone. She didn't have a dad that I knew of. Her name was Brenda. We played Atari games and played outside as well. On this particular day, we were playing with dolls in her upstairs loft. She asked me if I had ever been kissed. Children are so curious you know. I said no and asked her why she wanted to know. She said because she wanted to know what it felt like. Brenda was older than me by a year or two. So being ready to please because I just needed love I wasn't getting I suppose or perhaps just pure curiosity at that time, I let her kiss me. I didn't really like it one way or the other. I didn't know what was going on but what was to come next I truly wasn't ready for.

Brenda said, "Have you ever had sex?" I didn't know what the heck that was! So I said, "What is it that?" She went on to say that is was fun and that she would show me how it is done. So she stood behind me and pulled down my pants. She began to rub herself against me. Now, this was uncomfortable for me. Fortunately, we were quiet enough that her grandmother said, "What y'all doing up there?" She quickly dressed, and I did the same. She asked me if I could spend the night. I said I would ask my parents. We were a very close neighborhood. They all trusted each other I suppose. I spent the night.

That night while everyone was sleep Brenda got on top of me and pulled down my panties and began to grind on top of me. Skin to skin. Ok, we are Christians but let's keep it real from beginning to end. Deal? A lot of that made my body feel things I wasn't comfortable with and unfortunately, some things felt strangely good. I thought. Perhaps that is why somehow I thought I was wrong as well. Her mother came out of her room and Brenda stopped. I told her I didn't want to do any more of that. Of course, after that night I wanted to go over there more and I really didn't understand why then. I never told my parents about that. I had no idea if it was right or wrong. But instinctively I knew something wasn't right.

About a week later I was at another friend's house and she wanted to kiss me. She was beasty about it she said she would give me some perfume if I let her because I was saying no. She started and I was like yuck! Her breath was so funky my goodness. I was out of there. Now there were four of us that played together. Brenda and the other two were going to the 5th grade and I was going to the 4th. In my town I grew up in 5th and 6th grade were in the same school. Fourth grade was still in "Elementary." I guess I was still a baby. Anyway the next day they were all at Brenda's house. I rode my bike there as usual. I got there and they hurt my heart. They asked me what I was doing there. I told them I always come here because we always play together. Child I was dissed. Meaning, I got my feelings hurt. They told me to leave and don't come back. I left with my head hung very low in tears. Now I want to talk about Rob. The very next summer I was outside in my garage with my roller skates on playing with something. At this time I was going to 5th grade. Rob and about 4 other boys rode their bikes by my house. They lived in a neighborhood that was behind mine. It was truly considered a different neighborhood because there was a fence separating the house. Anyways, he stopped and spoke and I really had nothing to say. They were laughing and drenched with mischief. Now I don't know what they were up to but I didn't talk much and they eventually rode away. What happened next was so scary.

I thought they were gone so I went skating as usual. My house was on a corner. Picture my house on the corner of a rectangle. I was riding on the other street parallel to mine so I wasn't very far from home. I was halfway down the street when I noticed Rob and his group of friends, coming at me full steam ahead. Baby, I took off! We have got to keep our kids in shape. Praise God I was then. I got around the corner so I was heading down my street when I looked up and they were coming around the corner of my house! I was so scared. I stopped and turned around and went back the other way. My heart was pounding in my chest so hard I thought I was going to collapse. I got back to the other block and they were coming up that block. So we played that back and forth game until I was just about exhausted and ready to give up. I was nine or ten years old at this time.

So I kept riding toward them on the other street because my thought process was to get as close to them as I could without them catching me and then turn around and try to brake again. I did just that. So I got down my block as fast as I could. I was trying to make it to a house that I knew a retired couple lived that was about halfway down. I didn't make it I thought in time. So the house that I got to was a house that nobody was at home during the day. However, they had a huge van that sat in the driveway all the time. (I bet you know I don't ever complain about broken down cars in yards at all!) Now, this house had a double garage door. One of the doors was always lifted up just a little to show the very mean eyes of a dog that was so vicious I don't think I ever saw that dog. He was truly there to protect his home. He always, always barked when you just walked by.

Well, I ran up the driveway on skates and slid my body under that van. When I looked up that dog was looking dead at me. I started crying so hard without making a sound. My mom hated when I hid in the house. I could hide anywhere and never get found. I was so good at it. She hated it but God used it. I looked to my left and Rob and the boys rode by all cool calm and collected. They were enjoying this chase. I waited for them to get to the end of the block. I looked back at the dog that had been so very quiet for once in his life and got up and ran through the grass of the houses on skates toward my house. Jesus.

I got home and in the driveway. I sat in the garage sweaty and tired, scared and relieved. Those suckers rode by and halted when they saw me sitting there. I stared at them so hard I think they got scared. Perhaps Michael the angel was behind me giving them a piece of his mind. Glory to Jesus I never saw that boy again. I don't know what they would have done if they caught me. But after Brenda and the others and then him, I just wasn't sure. I don't know why but I never told my parents that either.

Dear Sis,

Sisters there are never rejections with God. Rejection is really His protection and direction. Had those girls never hurt my feelings I may not have had the snap to know that was a bad situation with Rob and his flunkies. Of course, I know the Holy Spirit was protecting me all along. I shared that story with my daughter when she was 7 years old. I just want her to know the truth. A little boy asked her to be his girlfriend the next year and she put her hand on his face and said, "Boy you better get away from me, and I'm a prophet and a child of God and no I don't want to be your girlfriend. My mommy says I am too young for that!" Yes!!!! See that is called breaking the cycle of a generational curse. We have to be real careful to share openly with our children. It is my deepest encouragement that we make our children understand and trust that they have a significant voice in the home.

I can remember several strong occasions where I tried to speak and no one took me seriously. No one listened to me on certain subjects that were critical and as a result, I stopped sharing or made up lies to try to engage my family. This was so unhealthy. Therefore when serious issues would arise I said nothing because I didn't think they would believe me or listen. Let me give an example.

I remember telling my parents about having extremely vivid dreams. I remember the first one was the Disney crew in court. Goofy was the judge, Mickey was the prosecutor, and Christ was the defendant. I remember Christ getting so pissed off because he was indeed guilty and turned into a horned creature resembling what we animate to be the devil. No kidding. That scared me so bad I wanted to run to my parent's room. When I got up out of my bed I looked down the hall and it looked like there were some people coming out of the walls. So I just stood there and tried to gather my courage. When I did I took off running full force. I burst into my parent's room screaming and of course, they were not ready to hear me because they had been asleep. God bless them. They didn't grow up knowing about prophets being formed at an early age, God speaking to you in dreams and the devil trying to distort what God is doing in your life. When I was saved I learned that God does just that with me. He clearly speaks to me in dreams.

I also know from that situation that the devil of fornication and homosexuality was after me from a very early age as we can see. I thank God that my mom had me in somebody's church. I thank God that he protected me in those days. We have to watch whose house our children are going to. Now don't go left on me. Find a good balance. We don't need to walk in fear for our children we just need to cover them in prayer and use godly wisdom. 2 Timothy 1:7 and Romans 8:15

Ephesians 6:10-18 amplified

In conclusion, be strong in the Lord [be empowered through your union with Him]; draw your strength from Him [that strength which His boundless might provides]. Put on God's whole armor [the armor of a heavy-armed soldier which God supplies], that you may be able successfully to stand up against [all] the strategies and the deceits of the devil. For we are not wrestling with flesh and blood [contending only with physical opponents], but against the despotisms, against the powers, against [the master spirits who are] the world rulers of this present darkness, against the spirit forces of wickedness in the heavenly (supernatural) sphere. Therefore put on God's complete armor, that you may be able to resist and stand your ground on an evil day [of danger], and, having done all [the crisis demands], to stand [firmly in your place]. Stand therefore [hold your ground], having tightened the belt of truth around your loins and having put on the breastplate of integrity and of moral rectitude and right standing with God, And having shod your feet in preparation [to face the enemy with the firm-footed stability, the promptness, and the readiness produced by the good news] of the Gospel of peace. Lift up over all the [covering] shield of saving faith, upon which you can quench all the flaming missiles of the wicked [one]. And take the helmet of salvation and the sword that the Spirit wields, which is the Word of God. Pray at all times (on every occasion, in every season) in the Spirit, with all [manner of] pray and entreaty. To that end keep alert and watch with strong purpose and perseverance, interceding in behalf of all the saints (God's consecrated people).

Chapter 1.5 – Safe at Home

I don't ever remember my mother and father telling each other they love one another. I mean to say I don't remember seeing them say it or act like it. I'm sure they did at one point in their lives. Anyway, so I had no clue whatsoever what love was. I did, however, learn about what a man was by watching my Dad. Unfortunately, it wasn't the right kind of man. I do not say that to bash, my father or mother. I love him and he has given his life to God and can easily say that he wasn't as good to my mother as he should have been. God gives everybody another chance. Therefore, I grew comfortable with what he showed me and looked for that kind of relationship without knowing. Meaning, I was more comfortable with a dysfunctional relationship than with a solid relationship with a really good man. I would chase after the wrong kind of man and totally reject a good man.

I learned about love through TV and the playground. It is so important that we teach our kids by not only talking but leading by example. There was no foundation of what love was or what it meant to be in love. Love cannot be achieved or understood without the love of Jesus first. God and Jesus show true love so when I say 'love' that is what I am talking about.

Talking about dating and the feelings that go along with that were not readily discussed with me as an adolescent. So dating snuck up on me and I was nowhere near equipped to make sound choices or apply real judgment.

Ok here comes the sticky part for me. I don't want to talk about this but I have to, at least briefly. I was way to nosey for my own good. I found porn tapes and sexually explicit magazines all the time. I am telling you that devil of lust is a generational curse after me. But it lost! Glory to God. Anyway as a child I had no business watching these things. If they were not in the house, I would not have watched them. I cannot tell you how important it is for you to protect your children from your own sinful weaknesses.

I was exposed to what cheating was by watching my parent's relationship. I love my father, however, growing up there were many times that I witnessed him inebriated. That was the time when we really spent a lot of time together. We would watch musicals and dance and act them out. I'm smiling because those memories were pleasant. Very happy actually. The not so good part is the morning after. He, of course, was hung over from the drinking. I would get him 2 aspirin and toast 2 pieces of breath with melted butter. So I learned how to take care of a man that was an addict, dysfunctional and handsome. I married a handsome dysfunctional addict which you will read more about later. My point here is to say that this warped way of thinking came at an early age. Again, please be careful what you are showing and teaching your babies.

I am making light of everything because I really don't think extreme details are necessary. I will say this. In addition to the manipulation and physical abuse inflicted by my sibling, the torture did go in a direction that no brother and sister should ever share. There were also many moments where I was locked in my closet when my parents were not home, beat up several times a week, verbalized every day and threatened. With that said, the point here is that I further learned about love from a man the completely wrong way. My Dad would come to my aid and try to hold my brother accountable but to no avail. When he went to college is when the beatings and abuse stopped – sort of – sadly the damage was done. Fathers and brothers are very influential in a young girl's life. What you say and do to them will shape their thoughts and focus toward men. That is so very real and so very true. I have had to undergo serious counseling for all my sibling inflicted in my life, verbal, physical, emotional and mental abuse lasted for the better part of my childhood into early adulthood. I will say that we are cool now. I try to see and accept his apology by how he handles me now, which is very well. I have forgiven him period. There is no other choice or way to live. Trust me.

This is dedicated to you and those of us who just don't have the courage to share the hardest parts. Please take this blank page to at least write out something you never want to share with anyone and get it off your chest. Much love.

Dear Sis

Chapter 2 – Foundation

So let me share my first experience with what I remember to be my first encounter with a 'good guy.' I wish I could use his real name because he was such a perfect boyfriend. I was only 12 when I met him and everyone at the baseball park knew that boy was sweet on me. He always showed up when my brother had a game. My brother was always excellent in sports so he was well known. My Dad made sure that we all had shirts that said Sister, Mom and Dad' which meant I was well known. Nelson, we will call him, always showed up with a red pop, blue bubble gum, and a snicker bar. That was my baseball game treats. He spoke to my parents. They had no problem with us sitting together or talking. Nelson would find me playing cup ball with the boys and whipping their butts at it! I always made better friends with boys for some reason. So when I became 13 I took Nelson seriously. Anyway, he bought me a tape player headset. That was big stuff in 1987. ☺ It had an automatic tape turnaround. Plus it was digital! Then he gave me a ring and necklace set that was gold. He was even considering buying me a moped. But here is the point.

Once I decided I would be grown and let him come inside my house after school one day. Well, I was curious and wanted him to kiss me and he did just that. He was so very uncomfortable though. I wanted him to press me up against the wall and he did, but he didn't want to and I insisted that he do so. I told him if he really loved me he would do what I asked. He told me if I really loved him I wouldn't do that though. He said you are better than that and I know your family and I don't want to do this. So I quit asking because something in me said he was being nice and I liked that. But I didn't appreciate it because you can't appreciate something you don't understand. It is kind of like when you are given or you are borrowing a car. You are not that concerned with how hard you close the door. You are not concerned with putting your purse on the car. You are not concerned with the condition of the tires. Honey but when you buy a car yourself you are very well interested in the tires and if the bottom of your purse has anything on it that will scratch the paint. In other words, you are completely aware.

Let someone close your door too hard, they will hear about it real quick! (Smile) There is a lack of appreciation when you don't know what you have in your midst.

So you see I didn't understand how wonderful it is that Nelson didn't go further than kissing me because he could have. Somehow between the incident with Brenda and finding a stash of porn flicks that I watched frequently, I developed a sense that when two were in love or liked each other that kissing and sex was supposed to be involved.

On my way to the ninth grade, I met a guy who I fell in love with so quickly. As most ninth graders do. I called Nelson and told him that I wasn't good enough for him. He cried and said he didn't understand why I was doing this. I said," you love me more than I love you and that is not fair to you. You deserve someone who will love you back." He was so hurt and devastated. I thought I was doing the right thing by not cheating on him. I really hurt him that day. I have since asked God's forgiveness for hurting such a good guy and pray that my actions didn't cause him to change.

Dear Sis,

If I would have seen an example of a good man which is a man of God I would have treated Nelson better. I am not sure as a teenager if I would have stayed with him because of obvious immaturity. But I am convinced that I would have respected him more. I thought that because I had treated a good guy so wrong that somehow I was being punished for it with all of the relationships that I was in that did not work that followed that one. This is hard to think about right now. I hate to remember when I actually hurt someone. God was not punishing me with all of those bad relationships that followed. I was making a choice.

I know that I needed a father that was a man of God to set a standard for guys that wanted to be my boyfriend so that I could see what was wrong and what was right. I love my father but it is the truth anyhow…..I just had to take a cry break. I told the Lord I can't believe I went through what all I am going to write about and someone is going to read about. I just thank God that He brought me through it all. If only 2 women read this book and their lives are changed, so be it. For that, I give God all the glory.

The better choice would have been to see all young men as my brother in Christ and not as a potential boyfriend. I was looking for the man of my dreams.

At that age? That should have been a foundation in Jesus Christ. He is the man of my dreams. What I needed was the comfort of a love that was so unconditional that I could really rest in that security. No matter how perfect or imperfect my parents were, they would never be able to provide the emptiness that drove me into the arms of men. That can only be cured by a relationship with Jesus Christ.

John 14:15 and 26 amplified

And I will ask the Father, and He will give you another Comforter (Counselor, Helper, Intercessor, Advocate, Strengthener, and Standby), that He may remain with you forever--But the Comforter (Counselor, Helper, Intercessor, Advocate, Strengthener, Standby), the Holy Spirit, Whom the Father will send in My name [in My place, to represent Me and act on My behalf], He will teach you all things. And He will cause you to recall (will remind you of, bring to your remembrance) everything I have told you.

Chapter 3 – The First Choice

This is the first man I truly acknowledged in my life as being really the man I was in love with. I met him at a church with a friend of mine. I guess I figured that is why he was so dog-on special. Satan's tricks are everywhere family. Anyhow, I thought he was shy and sweet. He was respectful and in the beginning, I believe he truly loved me. I was only 14. Please pick yourself up from off of the ground and stop laughing at me. You know you were in love too! Or at least you wanted to be in love. (Smile)

Peter, we will call him, had issues in his own home. I didn't know that of course at my age because my entire body was void of wisdom. Peter never tried to have sex with me either. That is another reason why he was so special. You know what, that is special at that age to respect a girl you like. Because I had no idea what a good guy was, I broke up with him for no reason as well. You might say that is so normal at that age. I was looking for mister right at that age. I could have married Peter and been so happy. I have always naturally been a one-man kind of woman. Whether you like it or not, we are concerned about boyfriends and girlfriends around that age. It starts younger now, but nevertheless, our hormones get going about that age.

I called Peter and told him I was interested in dating other guys and I didn't think it would be right to cheat on him. WOW!! He didn't take it well. I really hurt him. It took about 2 months for me to realize what a mistake I made. Girlfriends if you think you can just shove a good one around you have another thing coming to you. Our friendship never really was the same after that. I really believe he truly cared about me but this man never ever really took me back as his girlfriend. I basically chased him for the next 13 years. (About that much anyway) Oh yeah, I'm going to expose my ignorance so hopefully, somebody won't do this stupid stuff! Honestly, this chapter was so hard to deal with it took me 3 weeks to get up the nerve to write it since the previous chapter.

The truth is, I really loved this guy and with all my heart. I thought it was so pleasant to just be able to trust him, talk and share. I had my first kiss with this guy. Pleasantly speaking, it was wonderful. I was 15 and it happened when I walked him to his car outside of my home. I felt like I was on cloud nine. Let me say that it should not have happened because as a Christian believer I know that even a single kiss can open up soul ties that can have you bound. What is a soul tie? A soul tie is basically a spiritual connection to someone. When the phrase 'soul-tie' is used it is basically describing something unhealthy. Your soul is the part of your spirit that you have control over. You have to make the choice for your soul to be given to God and submitted to the example Jesus set forth for us. So if you tie yourself to something unhealthy it is very hard to break away. This is basically where habits are embedded in us.

Back to Peter. Let's move forward. After my high school graduation, I went to college. Lordy! We will get to that in the next chapter. I'm going to have to fast and pray to birth that one out. (Smile) Ok so now every time I came home for Christmas I would call Peter. Sure enough, he would come to see me. I thought I was so special because of this. He didn't bring a gift. He didn't come by himself. He always brought his homeboy with him. He didn't ask me for a date and court me like a special lady. He didn't pick me up and say let's go to a movie or bring me flowers or a Christmas card. He didn't even get dropped off to spend real quality time with me and my family. He just stayed for a while and visited and then left. I later found out he was hoping to get lucky and get some booty from me. I know we are Christians, but you understood beyond the shadow of a doubt what I just said, didn't you? Right. Let's move on.

Here it goes. The last time I looked in Peter's face it was 1996 or 1997. I don't really remember exactly which one. I thought about him because I was so lonely and figured I would try to find him. Well, I called information for the last city I knew he lived in. God allowed me to find him. Let me be very clear and say that God did not ordain that I find him though. What do I mean by God allowed this move? Please read 1 Corinthians 6:12. Paul clearly stated all things are permissible for me to do but that doesn't mean I should be retarded enough to do them. Well, Paul didn't say retarded, but I had to be to search for and find this dude. Trust me the devil takes much pleasure in orchestrating events to appear to be God and this was surely one of those moments. Sisters, nothing in the past clearly stated this man wanted to be with me, yet I was searching him out. The bible says that a man should find a woman. God is not an idiot; He knows what He means when

He says it. All the time, not some of the time, but all the time what God says is truly for our benefit. Y'all know he came to see me right? Let's just move one.

Remember I said I was lonely? **Lonely = desperate = sad = insecure = longing = weak minded = ignorant = naïve = addictions = unsure = worried = not doing anything with my life = open to satan's attacks = promiscuous = alone = desperate again = LACK OF THE LOVE OF JESUS CHRIST OF NAZARETH.** It is the truth anyway. He stopped by on his way home to Texas. See he wasn't even going to make a special trip to see me. And I thought I was so special. Baby, please! I didn't have hardly any money. I was eating because I had a job at a pizza place. When he arrived he didn't even hold me like I was missed. I ignored that because I was so happy he was there. It was a beautiful summer day. It was sunny, crisp and there wasn't a cloud in the sky. Sisters I was so broke I was not ashamed to say to him, "if you are hungry you are going to have to pay for food." So we went out to eat. We went to a fried fish buffet. After that, we went back to my apartment.

I had been having sex for the past 4 or 5 years so I was ready to get lucky with the man I loved. I am going to keep it real and you can receive it or not. If you don't know the love of Jesus, you don't know love at all. I am so serious. No one and nothing can replace the unmatchable love of Christ Jesus family. Sex is sex, whether copulating or oral, it is still sex. I guess I fantasized too much about the beauty of the first time he and I would make love that I figured in my warped mind that this was a beautiful thing about to happen. Girl, he didn't even make the first move. We lay down in the bed and I had just lost like 50 pounds so I thought I was the bomb! It was a really sexually charged environment thanks to my creative, romantic and lustful mind. He clearly expressed that he wanted foreplay before we did anything. Basically, he wanted me to perform oral sex on him. I did it. (Ok so now I know why I didn't want to write this chapter. I knew something in it would make tear up.) After I did the best job I knew how he was finished. No hug for me, no laying in the bed arm and arm, no anything. Oh, there was a goodnight. I think. I am not sure at all on that one as well.

Sad isn't it. What's really sad is I know some of you reading this have experienced the same exact thing. If you have not, please see the false signs that are being shown to you and stop ignoring them. Step back because you don't owe any man, anything. Unless he is your husband, you don't have to do anything for him to please him. I wrote him a letter and sent a picture of me. He didn't respond. When I went home a few weeks later, I called him. He didn't call back. He didn't call me because he didn't want anything but to satisfy himself. He didn't love me. He didn't like me. He just knew that I was weak enough to please him and not even kick his sorry (wait let me chill. I was about to say something crazy) behind out of my place. Sometimes I have to go off because I need that in my life to get my attention. After all those years, I finally got it. I said to myself, "I'm through chasing this man." I meant that. What I should have said was I'm through chasing men.

Dear Sis,

God says that a man should find a wife. Proverbs 18:22. I know that by heart because my husband now proclaimed it to the world when he found me. I love him.

I know what the problem is! We live our relationships in our fantasies. Seeing this awful men from our hopeful eyes instead of the eyes of truth and reality. We are lonely and don't want to be without love. I understand that but the main love we should never be without the love of oneself. I know it hurts to think about it all. Trust me. I know that we should never search for a man. So stop saying, "I haven't found my husband yet." You will never find your husband. It is God's responsibility to find him and present you to him. Peter was not the problem; and, he never told me he loved me and couldn't live without me. He did exactly to me what I let him do to me all because I was caught up in the fact that I first hurt him a long time ago. Somehow I may have been punishing myself for that fact. I was caught up in the fantasy that somehow we would have a happy life together if I just did whatever he wanted. Basically, I was lost and had no true love for myself or respect for myself for that matter. Ultimately, I did not have the love of Jesus in my life.

If a man will not love you the way God says, don't be confused or surprise when disappointment keeps invading your life. Love is not confusing. Yes, you have to work at it and work on your character flaws and he will have to work on his flaws. However, God's love does not breed disappointment.

James 1:13-16 amplified

Let no one say when he is tempted, I am tempted of God; for God is incapable of being tempted by what is evil and He Himself tempts no one. But every person is tempted when he is drawn away, enticed and baited by his own evil desire (lust, passions). Then the evil desire, when it has conceived, gives birth to sin, and sin, when it is fully matured, brings forth death. Do not be misled, my beloved brethren.

Chapter 4 – My First Time

I promise at one point in my life I was truly proud to be a virgin. In high school, all of my friends were not virgins and I was just fine with that truth. Knowing this never made me want to 'do it'. I remember once three of my friends and I went to pick up boys. I was driving. There was a boy for each of us. Now they knew their boyfriends but I didn't know the one they chose for me. When I first saw him I was so happy because he was so fine! My pastor, Betty Nelson, always tells us, women, "Be careful, otherwise, you will wind up with a fine devil!" That sounds so funny but it is so very true. Anyway, we went to the beach at night and by ourselves with four men. The Lord has been watching over me for a long time.

If I remember correctly the boys drove their own car because we could not all fit in my dad's car. When we first got to the beach we were having fun. The radio was playing and we were dancing and really having a good time. Well, the dancing turned to slow dancing and the boys got to grinding and the girls let them, including me. I really thought that part was ok because it wasn't sex. I bless God for my mother. She never had a lot of boyfriends. I believe my dad was her second boyfriend on her own and she married him at 19 years old. So there were never any real talks of what boys do to get sex from a girl. My dad didn't break it down although he should have and truly had the knowledge to do so. I'm going to leave that one alone.

One couple went into the car and got freaky. Two other couples laid down blankets in the sand and got freaky. Let me be clear. They began to have sex. Right there in front of me! I was stunned. So the boy with me came to me and wanted to get close. I guess that turd thought he was going to get lucky that night. Sike! While he was kissing me one of the girls came to me and asked could they use my car to get busy in. I clearly said no way. That immediately made me snap back to the reality that was surrounding me. The boy that was with me was so frustrated and disgusted because he was looking around at his friends getting what they wanted and he was not. I hollered out, "I'm leaving. If you want a ride to your house then get in the car and if you don't let these Negros take you home!"

I got my keys and I went to the car and got in. They hurried up because the car was started. I was going to leave them. I realized they had this whole thing planned and I was so naïve and they knew that I wouldn't know what was going on. What they didn't expect is that I can get pretty strong headed when I need to.

Needless to say, that ended that bogus friendship. I didn't really care either. It surprises me to remember that I didn't care because girlfriends meant everything to me back then. I will say that I really wish I had the kind of relationship with my parents that I could share those things so that they could tell me how it all works. But I thank God for what my parents did deposit in me because I eventually got it.

****

I am not sure how I got from virgin to being a straight up freak, but that is exactly what happened. I graduated shortly after that incident. I went to college still as pure as I could be. There was a guy that I met and we will call him David. I could not stand him. Actually I really favored his friend. Let's call his friend (you know what's funny is I really don't remember his real name) Mark. So Mark was tall, black and extremely handsome. I got nicknamed 'Baby doll' as my crab name at the University of my Dreams. My confidence had grown as a result and I had lost 25 pounds in band camp. I was a very solid 190 pounds. I was truly fine in my opinion because I was not 'fat'. We will talk about that later.

On my very first band trip to New York, I had a really interesting trip. I had not flown before so I was very nervous. I made sure that I was standing by Mark to get my plane ticket so that I could sit by him. You know who else was standing by Mark? You guessed it. David. I was not happy about that because he was purposely getting on my nerves. I had no idea that men get on your nerves when they like you. When I say he got on my nerves he really did! I was so aggravated by the time I got on the plane I forgot that I was nervous. That is until the plane started moving. I guess it must have shown all over my face because David was staring at me a little different now. I was sitting between him and Mark. Remember when I said I really liked Mark? Don't you know this dude had his earphones on and was listening to music? I know he knew I liked him because I made sure he knew. He must have smelled virgin on me because the only attention he showed me was that of a little sister and I was too stupid to see that fact.

David said to me, "Baby doll are you ok?" I was trying to be hard and said, "Boy yes I'm fine!" Then the plane stopped abruptly. I didn't know this was ok because the plane was just backing up to go forward again. David told me I could hold his hand if I like. He was surprisingly being so kind and sweet all of a sudden. I held his hand as the plane took off and I really needed to because I was so scared. We ended up talking the entire trip. I ended up getting to know him a great deal. He told me about his family and where he was from. He told me all about his career dreams. I learned he was a junior at the time and he was a leader in the band. I started to feel pretty good about myself that I could attract such a wonderful guy. This man was planning on being a doctor and had the grades and the character to achieve just that. The plane landed and by that time I had the biggest smile on my face. I really enjoyed spending time talking to the man. After we got off the plane, all of us went to get our luggage. David and I really didn't hang around each other to get our luggage. I hooked back up with my girls and waited for my luggage to come around the carousel. You were to go straight to the buses after you have gotten your luggage. There was always one band director waiting for everyone to get their items and make sure all were safely on the bus and out of the airport. I found myself standing there by myself wondering why my luggage was not in my hands and everyone else was on the bus. I told the band director my things were not there. I began to panic big time.

Time seemed to turn into slow motion as I realized the reality of my bag being missing. He called the airport officials and let them know it was missing. I wanted to cry so badly. My flute was in my bag. All of my uniform equipment was in the bag including all of my personal items. I was only 17 years old at the time. I was truly scared. I looked up while talking myself out of crying and there was David. I smile thinking about that now. I don't know where he came from but he was there. He and the band director went around handling business for me because I didn't know what the heck to do. Ultimately I had to file a report of what my bag looked like and what was in it so that they could locate my bag. We were told to go to our hotel and just wait there until the airport could fix their mistake. Because the band and football team were so hot and famous at the time I was assured they would really do their best to find my things.

It meant everything to me to march in the Band. I dreamed of going to that school all through high school. Because my high school band was like watching paint dry boring, I was so excited about the opportunity to march in the famous marching band. This would be my very first game to march in and I was pumped up a great deal. I spent a very hard summer working my butt off in band camp. I was the heaviest flutist and made sure I worked hard so that no one would want to challenge my spot on the field; which, means if someone is on the sideline and didn't get to make the field they could challenge your spot to try to take it from you. No one was going to do that to me because I was a very skilled flutist, I played with high volume, I marched fairly enough for a freshman and I was an excellent dancer. Now that you know all of this, imagine how a 17-year old that was finally about to live her dream felt when that seemed to come crashing down.

The band director, David and I got to the bus. Everyone was a bit irritated and hungry and was tired of waiting on the curly haired pretty girl who seemed to have snatched the attention of one of the most wanted boys of the band. I promise you I didn't see that at all then. Boy was I naïve to the real deal of the world. He sat by me on the bus and I really couldn't talk. It was pretty cool having someone by my side for once understanding me and just being there. I really didn't understand that though. I didn't understand how precious that was and how important it is to choose a mate that really has your best concern and not theirs in mind.

We got to the hotel and I was one of the last ones to walk in because I had to explain to every band director what the airport told me. I walked in and the first order of business was to get my room keys. While in line to get my room key, I looked in the banquet room where everyone was eating and I did not even feel like eating although I was so hungry. I was so upset I didn't want to go eat anyway. I just wanted to go to my room and cry. Wouldn't you know my name had not been added to the roster and I was not assigned a room? That was it I couldn't hold it anymore. I turned around and ran around the corner for privacy to cry. I was sobbing hard and then I heard a sweet voice say, "You need this?" When I looked up it was David holding a white handkerchief. I took it from him and began to calm myself down. He advised me to wait there for a minute. He came back and told me he arranged for me to share a room with his classmate which was one of the upperclassmen in my section and she happily agreed and gave me her room key so that I could go up. He also said that if I wanted to go to my room he would meet me there and check on me. I did just that.

Remember I said I thank God for my mother? Well, the bible says to train up a child in the way they should go and they will eventually return to that knowledge. (Proverbs 22:6 and Ephesians 6:4) Thank God she had me in a church. When I got to my room I found the bible and just picked it up. I didn't know anything about reading the bible because I grew up catholic and we used a missalette mostly. A missalette is a book that the catholic faith uses to read scriptures and follow the flow of the mass. I didn't know about calling on the name of Jesus. I didn't know that I could call that bag to be found by the power of the Holy Spirit. I didn't know that this was just life and all would be ok. I just opened it up and started reading somewhere. I don't remember what I read because I didn't understand a word the bible said back then anyway.

There came a knock at the door. It was David. He was carrying a tray with food, drinks, and dessert. My heart smiled so big that someone would take some time to consider me like this. We sat at the table and ate. We talked more and I began to feel better. He told me he had some things to do with the equipment and uniforms so he had to leave. He asked me if it would be ok for him to return later. I said yes so quick until it was funny! Smile.

Now the beauty of sharing a room with upperclassmen is they are never in their rooms. David did come back and he said let's go for a walk. I was scared because we did have a curfew to adhere to. He said it would be ok and let's just go. He took my hand and we went to the area where uniforms were kept. We spent the entire night up there. We didn't have sex but we did kiss. I saw the sun come up and panicked. He got me to my room and said good morning. I felt really special because this boy did not try to have sex with me and he had my back. Let me be clear really quick right here. I have matured into knowing that apart from God there is no good man. I believe that there would be a lot more really good godly men if the leadership in churches were more fearless about preaching the truth of God which not only includes His grace but judgment as well. We hang too much on the grace side which keeps us from honoring His complete righteousness. I said that to say it was good we did not have sex, but we should not have been alone unsupervised. We should not have kissed because that wakes up that urge to go further.

At breakfast, I guess the word had gotten out that David had catered to me and I got a few envious looks from some of the girls. Part of me was uncomfortable and part of me was happy. In the line to get my food one of the assistant band directors came and said they got a call from the airport and I needed to go to check on some things. I didn't get to eat and would not get to practice. I was not too happy about that either because we were doing a show with Jodeci and TLC and they were going to be at practice signing autographs and just hanging out with us. Dang! On the bright side, I got to ride with the world famous Eddie Robinson, the most winning coach in college football history, to the airport. Yes! That was so very cool. Even then God was putting me on true leadership so that I could begin to attach myself to it and smell the aroma of victory. The airport officials advised me that they had indeed found my luggage and I could come back and pick it up at a certain time. By the time we finished and got back to the hotel it was lunch time.

When it was time to go to the football game I had to ride with the band to the stadium first and then they were to take me to the airport which wasn't that far but far enough away that the driver had to hustle. We got to the airport and I got my luggage. Halleluiah! So I had to dress on a moving bus back to the stadium. This man had to be struggling because he came across as a nasty freak that was watching me in his mirror. I have never had the gift of truly holding my tongue so I told him if he didn't pay attention to the road I was going to wrap my flute around the back of his neck. Don't you know that turd laughed at me? Anyways, we arrived at the stadium and I was so geeked up and excited.

The same assistant that went with me earlier that day rode with me to the airport. Thank God because I didn't know my way around the stadium. We got off the bus and the assistant noticed that the bus driver had dropped us off on the opposite side of the stadium from where I was supposed to be. I had about 10 minutes to get around the stadium and down the shaft and to my position on the field to march the pre-game show. We took off running. We ran into a little girl on a stretcher who had passed out during the high school pre-game show. Her mother grabbed me and said please sign an autograph because it would make her baby feel so much better. The mother explained that it is her big dream to go to the same University one day. Of course, I completely understood that. I stopped to sign the autograph and gave her a big hug and told her she did a great job and keep up the good work and always protect herself first.

We took off running again. This stage was as big as the Reliant Stadium in Houston. HUGE! We ran through people and jumped over stuff. I felt like I was flying. We ran down the shaft and someone yelled, "She's supposed to be over there, go!" He pushed me in that direction. I looked to my right and saw the drum majors entering the field to start. I don't know where I got more steam from but I exploded. I found my section and said, "I got it!" to the assistant and he stopped and bent over in exhaustion. I ran up to my spot and as soon as I got there those six whistles to begin to blow out from the field and the drum majors. I came to attention and went out blowing my horn! No kidding. I had zero time to be nervous about my first time marching. It was so loud in that stadium. The crowd went wild. It was a fabulous experience that I truly treasure.

****

David and I were able to see each other on band trips following that. We did not engage in sex at a time because we were just chilling out together. I had a lot of fun with him. This is a funny part. I had my 18th birthday that September and it was now the latter part of October. It was time for the Cotton Bowl Classic in Dallas, Texas. Home! My parents were coming and at that time my brother was playing for Prairie View A&M. I was happy that I would get a chance to see them all because I had not seen them since the summer time. My parents found me in the stadium and came over to hang out with me. That was so fun. They told me that they would come to my room to hang out with me for a while before they headed back to Houston. So after the game, I found my brother to say hello and we talked for a quick minute. We whipped them 53 to 3 so he really wasn't in the mood for talking. We didn't have a good relationship then anyway.

When I got to my room my roommate had company. I always made friends with guys much better than girls so I was pleased that I only had one roomy and she was very freaky so she never ever stayed in our room. I almost always had the room to myself. Some of my crab brothers and David were there in the room. One of my girlfriends came with me so she could meet my parents. When I got in the room I said, "Y'all better get the heck out of here! My parents are coming to visit me." I didn't want my parents to think I was just freaking out or something. They had already begun cutting hair in the bathroom so it was hard for them just to pack up everything. Another one of my girlfriends was in the bathroom helping. Right then a knock came at the door. My friend said it was my parents! We all panicked.

We closed the door and hoped that they didn't have to use the bathroom. David stayed out and sat at the table. The other 4 guys were in the bathroom. Oh my goodness. (Smile) So my parents came in and sat down and fellowshipped with us for a while. Then an awful crash came from the bathroom and they all flooded out. I must have turned burgundy! My parents were just cool enough to introduce themselves and continue talking like it was all good. Ok so let's break and discuss that. I appreciate them for not embarrassing me, but it may have been a good idea to talk to me outside and say be careful not to let a guy take you too far. I believe my parents figured that I was in college now so what I chose to do was fine as long as I did what I was supposed to do with my grades and responsibilities. That is true however we are Christian people. Part of that responsibility is maintaining my walk as a Christian child of God. My parents didn't talk to me about these things. I don't blame them because it was not taught to them. It being purity based on God's way. My mom always told me about waiting until I got married but she stopped talking after I graduated. Still, I don't blame them, this is just how it happened and God allowed it for a purpose.

After my parents left David kicked everybody out. I suppose that was their chance to minister to me by quickly saying something to remind me that I was a woman of God. Knowing my personality, if it were my children I would put the boys out as I left and give my children a quick reminder of who they are in Christ. Here again, we only teach what we know. It was now our time to hang out by ourselves. That was the night we did have sex. He was completely gentle and sweet. He was completely loving and he stayed there after it was over and held on to me tightly and expressed that he did care about me. Let's take another break here. Again I say, apart from God, there is no good man. David treated me very well in his thoughts and in mine as well. This is the problem with doing things outside of the will of God. Because it doesn't line up to His instructions, there will always be a level of confusion that enters in. I was nowhere near mature enough to handle that kind of relationship. Although I consider David one of the best boyfriends I have ever had, he wasn't mature enough for me either.

I began to complain about us not spending more time together. I complained about everything. I wondered why he wouldn't show me more attention in band practice. He explained he was a pre-med major and he was a band leader and he didn't have time to see me during the day because he was busy studying. He couldn't hang too much in band practice because it wasn't appropriate being that he was a leader. He was right about all of that. But I didn't see that. I broke up with him because I was never ever going to be treated like my mother got treated. I would never let a man treat me bad. I would never just exist in a relationship. I have to take a cry break. Oh, Lord Jesus. I hurt him. I hurt him really bad. I didn't know it. I thought I was protecting myself from being hurt.

Don't you know confessing extremes such as, "I will never," will take you all the way to the other side of what you say? Which means you will do it anyway. I had no idea at all what a good man looked like. I didn't grow up seeing one. My father was a great dad as far as sharing his time with my brother and me. He completely encouraged us in our gifts. I love him for that. However, he did not show me how a man should treat a woman ever. He did not explain to me how I should be treated and He most definitely did not show me in his actions toward my mother. I love my Daddy. The truth doesn't always sound good, but it still is the truth. I believe if given the chance David would have really made me a great boyfriend and maybe even more. In God's sovereign plan He allowed my ignorance to break apart from something that could have been special. I have nothing bad to say about David but only to account for my promiscuous actions that should not have taken place.

Dear Sis,

I should not ever have been with him alone like that. We should have never been sleeping in the same bed on all those band trips. I should not have had sex with this man. I should have waited for marriage. I did not know that David was a good guy. I did not know that he was not out to hurt me and he was out to love me. Years I later found out that he was talking to his mom and telling her that he thought that he had found his love. I couldn't receive that because I didn't know what a good man was back then. I had no example. I did not know anything about dating or courting.

What I learned is that because I was so familiar with the wrong way to be loved that I could not recognize the right way to be loved. The right way involves closeness with Jesus Christ and a disposition to live a life according to the gospel. That reality ultimately scared me. It scared me to see opposite of what I knew. I knew the wrong way. I was familiar with the wrong way. The wrong way was comfortable to me. I was so close to my daddy. I picked up a lot of his habits and I grew comfortable with the man he was and the man he showed me. My Dad struggled with alcoholism big time and I saw him drunk a lot. That would eventually play a huge role in my decision making and in my choices in men. We always sang songs together and pretended to perform in front of people. That was my happy times with him. My father never missed any recitals or performances growing up. That was very special and still is special to me. Still, I heard the arguments and the cruel words flowing to my mother and from my mother to him. I found his porn stash and I watched it. I sneaked in his cigarette stash and smoked them. I started both of those around 8 or nine years old. I sure do hate that this is all true. My pastor always says what we do in moderation our children will do in excess. That is such wisdom and truth.

I grew very comfortable with the wrong things very early. So when it was time for me to start making decisions for myself completely I made them based on what I knew. I don't know what else to say. Perhaps thank God for His unchanging word and love toward us.

Zephaniah 3:17 amplified

The Lord your God is in the midst of you, a Mighty One, a Savior who saves! He will rejoice over you with joy; He will rest in silent satisfaction and in His love He will be silent and make no mention of past sins, or even recall them; He will exult over you with singing.

Chapter 5 – Wilding Out

I will not labor your reading time with a bunch of my indiscretions and tell you all the stories but will give you some examples. Isn't it cool how we can say things that make sin sound nice like indiscretions? Let's call it what it is – sin – downright nasty sin. I think I spent the next 14 years of my life hoping to find something as beautiful as David and I had together. I really can't say that for certain but I know I was hoping for something that special. I became very promiscuous.

I met a guy through a girlfriend of mine. Let's make this quick. This man had an orgasm while inside of me and looked me in my face and said, "I didn't know I was coming." I believed him. I didn't know any better. I remember telling my dad what happened and he said, "That punk is lying! Vawn, every man knows when that is happening." I felt so stupid. I was pregnant. I ended up going to the hospital for terrible cramps about one month later. The nurse and doctor in the country of Louisiana treated me like a nasty little black whore. I remember the nurse tried to give me a catheter. I couldn't bare it. She got frustrated and snatched the tube out of me. That night I had told my mother what happened. She cried and was scared at the same time. Still she loved on me.

The nurse and doctor told me that the cramps were not a problem as long as I didn't start hemorrhaging. They didn't bother to explain to me what that was so I left the hospital as ignorant as I came in. I ended up bleeding for 18 days straight. By the time I got home at the Chris break, which was about 23 days later, my dad knew what was going on. He took me to a clinic to have an abortion and I wouldn't calm down enough for the doctors to do anything. I was scared and I felt stupid still. Remember what I said about walking outside of God's will always leads to confusion? Well I was cross-eyed in confusion now. My mom took me somewhere to get the procedure done. This place was much nicer and the doctors were so much kinder to me. They examined me and found that there was nothing in me anymore. They explained that all of that bleeding was my body miscarrying the baby. He was stuttering because he said I should have been dead. He said that I was a lucky little lady and I needed to be careful.

I was relieved, scared and confused all at the same time. I began drinking more than usual. I decided not to go back to school for the spring. I could not handle that. The whole spring of 1994 was a blur. I got into trouble with the law and I slept with almost every guy that crossed my path. My father and I had an extreme argument once. We were so loud when I walked out of the house the neighbors were outside looking. I left and got me a hotel room. I called home to check on my mom and she said when you are not here he takes it out on me so please come back home. I came home. This is really difficult to revisit and write. But as we prayed in the beginning, we are all on this journey together.

****

I went back to University the fall of 1994. I left to get away not to get an education. Ultimately that is what happened. I did not get my education. I had several relationships that were strictly booty calls. I thought that I was meeting my husband each time I met someone new. At least that is what I was hoping would happen. In 1995 I met this guy and I completely don't remember his name. Let's call him Chris. Chris was cool and sweet. Chris sold drugs. I didn't know much about that. I just knew that I should never do drugs. I always consider drugs to be stuff you sniffed up your nose and shot up your arm. This dude sold weed – marijuana.

I didn't try it until I got back from visiting my mom. I moved my mom out of the house I grew up in that spring. I remember my dad telling me the reason she left was because of me and my brother constantly butting in and reminded her of the problems. I cried that day when I left him and I had received that it was my fault. I did tell my mom a lot of what I saw. I told her in 1994 when I found out my dad was cheating on her with my best friend's mom. I went to visit that woman too. I sat on her sofa and asked her why. She said she was lonely and that her husband died a few years before and my dad treated her nice. My dad said to me that I couldn't understand because there was no affection between him and my mom. I was thinking, "I wonder why you nut!" Even though I saw my Dad's faults I am mature enough to know it takes two to make a marriage work. That is not to say my mother deserved being treated that bad, but it does take two. And sometimes, the other need to run like hell is after them from that relationship, and that's what it took. Got me? Anyway, I received everything my dad told me.

I tried the weed in 1995. It made me laugh and have fun. I laughed so hard until I stopped crying all the time. I tried it again about 2 months later and I really got high. I really liked the feeling. It made my body feel so relaxed. I loved the fellowship of smoking weed. We would play dominoes and listen to music all night. We all laughed and talked. That summer I was dating Chris and a guy we will call Joseph. I was having sex with both of them. I really liked Chris because at the time I thought he was a 'good one'. He was caught up with a girl back home and had just found out that he got her pregnant so I knew we could never get serious. He said he had to choose her because of the baby and said he hated he had to make that choice but he has to do the 'right thing.' I still kept seeing him. My choices in men began deteriorating drastically at this time being my thought process was distorted. I couldn't tell crap from the cake. I found out I was pregnant in July. I went to the abortion clinic. I told Joseph it was his. I didn't know which one but I am pretty sure it was Christ. Remember what I said about walking outside of God's will always bring you confusion? Now I was smoking confusion. After I had the abortion I went back home. I called my mom and said, "Hi mom. I just got through having an abortion and I wanted to let you know." I didn't say it like I was proud because I was not happy about what happened. I always did have a desire to be a great mother one day, I hoped.

****

That fall I got with this guy who would give me anything. I was hoping he would be the one too. I don't know where he got his money from but he had it. I would go over and smoke and get zooted out of my mind and eat as much as I wanted to eat and have as much sex as I wanted to have. I am not proud of my past so I have to take a break.

Ok. Danny and I were cool. He was a 'good guy' too. So I really didn't like him that much. I always thought something was wrong with him. I still hung on him though because I wanted to stay high and I didn't have money. The devil always did make it completely easy for me to stay high. I went to class high. I went to my little part time job high. I remember one night Danny had a party. I just knew I was special because he told me to pick all the music I wanted to hear. I have always loved music so much so I was ready to fulfill that request. Everyone came to the party ready for a good time and that's just what we gave them. I invited a close friend of mine at the time to the party. She was just as depressed and jacked up as I was but I didn't notice. We got so high we had to go outside for a minute and giggle all over ourselves. Danny came outside and wanted to know what we were doing. I don't remember what was said I just know he courted me by giving me and my friend a blunt to ourselves to enjoy outside without having to share with anyone inside.

About December that same year, my friend invited me to her house. She told me she had some serious things to talk to me about. I was really nervous about that so I made sure I was good and high before I got over there. She had prepared dinner and we ate and talked. The whole time I was uncomfortable so I said let's blow. We did. Finally, I pressed her to tell me what this was all about. We had been hanging together almost every day that fall and grew really close. She said she had something to tell me about Danny. I thought she was going to tell me he had AIDS or something the way she was crying and trying to build up enough courage to express whatever she had to say. I screamed, "Come on tell me what's up!" She said, "Me and Danny have been sleeping together and I am so sorry but I love him."

I looked at her in eye to eye and said, "Well that's it then, it isn't it?" I went to an astray and got the rest of the blunt that wasn't smoked, I got my coat and put it on, I put fire to my blunt and took a puff and I looked at her and walked out the door. That was it for her and Danny. I went home and cried and got high again. So much for him being a 'good guy'.

****

By the time I met Pete I was smoking maybe 6 or 7 blunts a day. This was the spring of 1996. I was now 265 and wanted to lose weight. So I did. I got down to 215. I really thought Pete loved me. I would even talk to his mom. I went to visit him and all we did was have sex in a hotel. That turd didn't even buy my lunch. I was such an underpaid whore. One day I talked to his mother pleading with her to make her son love me and she told me, "get down on your knees and ask God to remove the love you have for my son because baby he does not want you." While that slapped me in the face and kicked a whole in my heart, because I spent one year getting to know this guy, that truth got me away from him.

So I moved on. One night while I was coming home from a weed session I ran into Shelton. (That's what I am going to call him) Shelton said something to me to get my attention. I remember saying something like when I find a good man I will let you know. This dude followed me upstairs. To make this story short, we started dating. The fun thing about this guy is he knew how to tame the lion in me. He could watch me be my normal bold and vivacious self and not be intimidated at all. I loved that about him. He was a fly dresser and just truly into me. We had a great time hanging out. I am making this story really short because what really matters about Shelton comes later. Basically, I started to love this guy. We started sharing ideas and dreams in between sex and getting high. He listened to me and he really understood me. I could be all myself and he encouraged the great things I thought about like performing and singing.

One day I dropped by his apartment like I always did to hang out. I walked in and it looked like he was packing. I asked what was going on and he told me he was moving. He said, "Sweetie I am graduating." He said that so happy. My heart sunk to my shoes. It must have shown because he stopped what he was doing and came to hug me and asked me if I was happy for him. I was really happy for him. Now I knew that we could never be together for real. We had just started dating a month prior. He asked me if there was something I needed to say to him and I just said that I was proud and happy for him. I didn't have the courage to tell him I was hoping he would be my husband and that I was falling in love with him. He didn't have the courage to say he was really digging me as well. It was too soon in our friendship to go there anyway. So he graduated and left. I felt let down again by love and life. I began to wonder why is it when I start to like a man, I mean really like a man he seemed to run away from me. It kept happening over and over again.

****

I remember once I met this guy while I was about to go into my apartment. He had huge glasses on his face and one of the eyes did its own thing. No kidding. He told me how beautiful I was and I thought this dude was really courageous. To make this story short, I considered hanging out with him because I was so not attracted to him on first glance. I thought that was shallow and if he is nice I should at least give him a chance. Of course, he had weed on him and that made the deal much sweeter. Well, one night about 3 am there came a knock at my door. I went to open the door and there stood, in the nighttime rain, a tall, skinny and pale man in a tan trench coat.

As he flashed open his coat and sucking his top two good teeth said, "Say, girl, you know you want this. Girl, I know you are in love with me. I felt you percolating for me!" I am so serious. As I checked him out from head to toe and noticing his white boxers with red hearts on him I almost wanted to laugh. Instead, I said, "Boy no! You better get out of here and don't ever come back here anymore!" I thought to myself, even the cross-eyed ones are crazy!

The truth has I had way too many encounters and sexual encounters. I don't know why I thought that having sex was going to get me close to my husband. I saw other women with good men by their side and they didn't even appreciate them. I would think to myself of how good I would be to them if they were my man. I was a lost, jumbled up and a hot mess. Seasoned women need to talk more to young women in an open real way so that they can get good information that may not be in front of them to grasp. I always think that if I just had someone to keep talking to me, someone to be in my face fearlessly, and someone I could really open up to in a real way perhaps I would have snapped into some sense. I really didn't want to burden my mother with my mess and as much as I love her we have never been able to talk about men. Bless her heart and thank you, Jesus, she didn't have that much experience. Again I say I thank God she didn't because I could have ended up worse. I am saying all of us that are women of God need to allow young women to talk to us about whatever they are concerned about and keep it real with them so that they can gain our wisdom early. Let's move on.

****

Remember David my first? We had been working at a group home. I remember seeing him one day while we were outside with the kids. This was the week after Shelton graduated. We began to talk more and more. I started to remember how much I loved him and how stupid I had been to let him go. Love had offered nothing but disappointments since he and I dated 4 years ago. I could trust him so we talked about a lot of things including my love life. I shared this with one of my lovely girlfriends. We had been friends since we were roommates in band camp. I love her even now. Her boyfriend and David were fraternity brothers.

David and I had a chance to really grow to love each other again. He loved me more like a friend that he could love for a lifetime and I loved him like I was hoping we could get together again. We spent a lot of hours at work watching the kids play and sitting down just talking again. I learned how goofy I was for breaking up with him by just enjoying his company more than anyone since him. One day in the summer I was having a pretty good day. I got a call early that morning from my girlfriend's boyfriend saying David was is a very bad car accident with another one of our friends. The friend in the car had died and David was in critical condition and they didn't know if he was going to make it. I don't guess I need to say how empty I felt. I really couldn't breathe and I called a friend of mine to come over because I thought I was going to pass out. She came and we got high while I stopped my life and waited something to tell me. At that moment a beautiful brown woman walked through the door and went to the other side of the bed and bent down and kissed him on the mouth. I was so stunned I couldn't speak or move and I continued to hold his hand. He said, "Baby doll, this is my fiancé." I smiled and gave a normal smile knowing I had missed out. I told her I was pleased to meet her and that I was so happy for her. I was you know, because the way I saw it, somebody deserved this precious man. If it wasn't me it should be somebody. I just cried because I couldn't be fake. It hurt so very much. Oh Lord it hurt so much. I told them I hope they have the most beautiful life together and I looked at her and told her I will always love your man but I love, love so much that I would never be a problem. I kissed him on the cheek and left. I was so hurt I didn't want to be high. I just wanted him to be my husband. That sounds so lost and crazy. I am laughing at myself now.

When I left the room I found my friend and we left and I told her not to talk to me just drive me home. The next day I left early to go to the hospital to visit with him. I saw a lady with rollers in her hair and she said, "Hey baby," in a really southern accent. I sat down by her and smoked a cigarette. She asked me was I there visiting family. I told her I was there getting closure for myself and visiting a man I once wished was my husband. I felt that my way of moving on was to see him recover. She said she understood. I looked up into the sky and noticed it was as blue as God must have wanted the sky to blaze. It felt so good to be a summer morning. As we set on the bench she began to explain to me that her son was in a near fatal car accident. I know right? It seems a trip that God would allow me to sit by a woman that would never be my mother in law. I can only laugh right now through these tears.

I said, "Well it's my pleasure to meet you, my name is Vawn Gretta." She took off her shades slowly and looked at me up and down and said, "Vawn Gretta Stearnes?" No kidding. This woman sat next to me and said my whole name and all I knew was her last name. We sat there and talked about her son. She told me about how proud she was of him and how the president of the university had come the day before to help them with whatever they needed. She said that I should be the one to marry her son because he loved me first. She asked me why I left him alone and I told her the truth. I was stupid and immature and didn't know what I was doing. I told her that David had always been a gentleman to me and always made me smile. I told her she may as well love her new daughter in law because I was never going to cause confusion for him because I loved him that much. She said, "You ain't ever lying girl." I laughed on the inside. I love her too. She gave me her number and address and told me to check in on her from time to time. I did check on her right before Katrina hit and we talked for a while. I would never ask David to call me because I wanted him to be happy and I know he loves his wife and I know I wanted him so I needed to stay as far away from him as I could.

So I went to see him one more time and said I know you are going to get well so I won't be back. He understood. He always understood me. We did see each other at work after he got well but I never made myself available to talk to him intimately again. One day he came over to me and asked me if I would hang out with him that night because it was his last night in town. I told him yes. He came to pick me up and we went around town going from one fight party to the next. We really had a good time laughing and singing like goofy people. The same fun we had before in the past. It really was beautiful. The night grew late and it was time to go home. David brought me home and came into my apartment to make sure I had gotten there safely.

We sat on the sofa and talked more. We also listened to music. He then grew close to me and kissed me. I felt like I was being kissed by a king or something. There is no such thing as an innocent kiss but that was one of the safest ones I have had in my lifetime. He said to me that he appreciated my friendship and knew that we wouldn't see each other anymore because he was headed to live his adult life. He wished me well and then he left. I watched him through my blinds get to his vehicle, get in and then close the door. That was it. He was gone and gone forever. I felt like my chances of having a good man in my life were gone forever. I blamed myself for breaking up with him at that moment. I received that I just didn't deserve a good man and should be happy with whatever I got. I suppose that was the beginning of me punishing myself and accepting whatever came my way.

Dear Sis,

I know I wish I had a mature woman in Chris to talk to. (Smile) Perhaps I would have been told that God doesn't make mistakes. If He wanted me to be with that man He would have made that happen. I would have been told not to blame myself because I was young and all young women break up with men for no reason sometimes. So there was no reason for me to blame myself and begin to torture myself physically and spiritually behind something that wasn't in my destiny to become anyway.

Sisters, we can't get mad at ourselves for past choices. We have to accept what we have done and move on quickly. We have to try not to make the same mistakes and move on. If we don't, the devil will play our poor choices over and over again in our heads; and, that leads to a lot of issues that will harm us. Issues like depression, obesity, laziness, and all kinds of addictions. I began to eat and smoke day and night. I drank liquor like it was going out of style too. I drowned my sorrows in something that only made those sorrows magnify. It is a lie to believe that weed is not a drug. It is the most damaging because it can lead to others real easy. If the devil would have gotten me close enough to be with the other drugs at certain points in my life I would have done them real quick. Thank God for Jesus.

David was not my man. God did not want him to be my husband. If He did God would have made that happen. I want to express clearly that we are not to hang on to the past. When a relationship is over, it's over. Don't go backwards. God moves forward and we should move forward with Him. Don't be a psycho chick and go after the man and his woman. I don't care if he was yours first, he is not now. Don't sit there depressed because you don't have a man. As we keep going you will soon discover why I say that and we will uncover the truth about how we should see ourselves and respond to what happens in our lives. Remember, it's all for purpose. Forgive yourself for your poor choices and others for how they treated you real quick as well so that you can live.

2 Thessalonians 2:3-12 King James

Let no man deceive you by any means: for that day shall not come, except there come a falling away first, and that man of sin be revealed, the son of perdition; Who opposeth and exalteth himself above all that is called God, or that is worshipped; so that he as God sitteth in the temple of God, shewing himself that he is God. Remember ye not, that, when I was yet with you, I told you these things? 6.And now ye know what withholdeth that he might be revealed in his time. For the mystery of iniquity doth already work: only he who now letteth will let, until he be taken out of the way. And then shall that Wicked be revealed, whom the Lord shall consume with the spirit of his mouth, and shall destroy with the brightness of his coming: Even him, whose coming is after the working of Satan with all power and signs and lying wonders, And with all deceivableness of unrighteousness in them that perish; because they received not the love of the truth, that they might be saved. **And for this cause God shall send them strong delusion, that they should believe a lie: That they all might be damned who believed not the truth, but had pleasure in unrighteousness.**

Chapter 6 – Confusion Depends

My time spent at the University was not all about men and failed relationships, however, for the purpose of this book, these are the subjects that we must visit. I performed a lot around campus and throughout Louisiana. I became pretty popular in the performance circle. I had a really good time acting and singing and putting together recitals. I learned that stage was truly my passion. I really didn't know what God was up to back then but He was depositing skills in me knowing that I was an immature knucklehead at the time. I barely went to classes but I never missed a practice or performance. Like I said in the beginning of my University days, I went to college to get away not to get my education. If it wasn't for all of the life skills I learned and musical achievements I gained, it would have been a total waste of my life. In the fall of 1997, my life would prove to change forever.

I can tell you right now that nothing in me wants to revisit or even share where we are about to go right now but I know it is for a purpose. I am praying that becoming completely transparent will cause many sisters to choose differently. I am praying that ultimately it will press my sisters to choose God first and not waiver. Well let's get to it, shall we?

The spring of 1997 was pretty cool. I was dating someone and for the sack of keeping his identity private, I will say that he was a musician. This was cool to me because we were both fairly popular and it was like a dream college romance in our circle of people. I did begin to really like him a lot. I thought he was cool enough. I think I have always loved way too hard and so it has always been hard for me to find a balance. I would even pretend to understand that fact. Like how do you love a little? Shouldn't we love with everything we have? Well, as long as it doesn't supersede the love we have for ourselves. Let's move on.

For some reason, I thought again that this guy could possibly end up being my husband. Therefore I made myself available to him at any time he wanted me to be available. Let's take a break right there. Honey, listen to me. Do not ever make yourself more available for a man than you make yourself available for God. If you do then he becomes an idol. One of the commandments tells us not to worship idols. (Exodus 20:4-5) I remember once I went to his place to hang out. I usually would never let a man pick me up because I wanted to be in control of being able to leave when I wanted to. But because I felt like he was a 'good guy', I figured I could trust him. Trust only God because the bible tells us that we should put our trust only in Him. (Psalms 146:4-5)

So on this particular night we were beginning to get intimate and he reached his climax before we even began so he was highly embarrassed. He decided he wanted us to go into the living room and smoke a joint so that we could chill for a minute and then go back to where we left off. After the joint we were still sitting there and I became concerned. So I told him that he should not worry because that happens sometimes. He got nasty with me and said that I needed to shut up and just sit there. I raised my eyebrows as if to say, "I know you didn't just go there with me!" I did tell him, "Look man, I did not come over here to just sit here and watch ESPN with you so if that is all you want to do then you can just take me home now!"

No kidding this thang looked at me and said, "I will take you home when I get ready so just shut up, shoot!" Of course he did say 'shoot'. So I told him, "Boy I don't know who you think I am but I don't need you to get me home sucka I can walk." I got my stuff and left. I left at 3am and walked home in the country. It was very dark and there were hardly any street lights. My place was about 10 minutes or so driving time away, not including traffic lights. About ten minutes later I got to a store and used the pay phone and God had a ram in the bush for me. My girlfriend actually woke up and she came to pick me up. That was it for him. There is always protection in God's directions. He didn't want me in that situation anyway so He provided a way out for me even in my sin. Despite what we call grace, this is really grace. I didn't deserve this protection, but He gave it to me anyway. Be careful of how you see rejection. Rejection can be God's protection and His direction. Of course anything could have happened to me on the street that night so I give God the total glory for protecting me again.

****

Before I get to the meat of where we are going let me tell you something about that summer. See when you are chosen of God, His protection is on you for only one simple reason. That reason is because He loves you. When I give

God glory I just can't believe sometimes how He was protecting me in my ignorance. In the summer of 1997 I began to get so desperate for money because there were so many students needing part-time jobs they were very scarce. I finally decided to drive 30 miles away to try to gain employment. It worked because I began to work for a pizza place as a server. That job barely paid anything but it was a job nonetheless. I would get tips breaking the scale at $0.43. I had a good job at the children's home but I was fired from that job. So basically I did have a good job but had absolutely no integrity to keep that job.

My apartment management was threatening to evict me and I had nowhere to go. I was engaged in a conversation about this one guy who I knew pretty well. He was a musician and I saw him all the time over the years. He had a girlfriend that he lived with and everyone knew how much he cheated on her. I always knew that for myself but on this particular day someone I knew was reminding me of how much money he had and that I should talk to him. Apparently, she had 'talked' to him before and that sounded like a good suggestion. I would like to be very clear right now so that there is zero confusion. I would need to engage him about sleeping with him for money. That sounds so good, doesn't it? Let's call it what God calls it. I was to talk with him about fornicating and joining myself to a harlot by prostituting myself. I am biting my bottom lip right now. This is one of those areas that I really don't want to share and that I am thanking God that He loved me enough to protect me this time.

I did talk to him about it and he accepted it and was very happy about the opportunity to give me what I was asking for. I was watching the movie "Soul Food" and I had a thought about asking family for help. I called my mom and she was completely against the idea she told me of different things family members were going through and that I shouldn't bother them. Of course, she had no idea what I was planning in a week. I have to ask for forgiveness again right now because I did write my uncle. I was so scared about becoming a paid whore you see. The day I was to go and see this guy I checked my mail and there was a letter there from my Uncle. I have always been afraid to tell him the truth of what he did for me. I can only pray that he will still consider me special.

I had asked my Uncle for $200.00 because I had $75.00 for the rent. My rent was $275.00 back then for a small one bedroom apartment. When I looked at the letter I was so happy. I was really happy that he sent me a letter and was not expecting any money in the letter. If there was no money in the letter I would not have been mad or become bitter with him I was just so happy he took the time to write me. Really. He explained how he understands family is important and he thanked me for my honesty. I told him in my letter that there was no way I would be able to pay him back and that I was truly just asking for the money. He ended it by saying he loved me and then I looked at the check. It was written for $500.00. I did not spend one dime of that money on weed. I was proud of myself for that. By this time I had begun to feel like I shouldn't be smoking it but I couldn't seem to stop.

I praise God for my Uncle. He will never know how God truly used him to stop me from doing such an awful thing to myself, to my God-given temple, and to my precious, fearfully wonderfully made body which is not my own but God's. Thank you, God. I need to take a cry break and a praise break.

****

One somewhat chili night a girlfriend and I were at my apartment getting high and listening to music. We were having a fairly good time. She decided she wanted to see her boyfriend who lived on campus. Jesus. Just thinking about how all this started is really messing with my insides. Anyway, we went to campus to get something to eat first. There were several choices, several meanings like five! Smile. We chose a po-boy shop to get something to eat. I think I had an oyster and shrimp po-boy. Don't ask me what she had because I was very high. I am guessing on mine because I wouldn't eat anything else.

For some reason, I thought that I had conquered some issues in my life because I was able to successfully lose 50 lbs. I thought because I had lost that much weight and was attractive again that I could attract a really 'good man.' We drove over to the dormitory where this guy was living and we parked. She went in to get him to come out and I waited in my car while eating my sandwich. Eventually, my, friend came back the car and she and her boyfriend were just visiting. While we were sitting in the car someone came by my window and knocked on the window really hard and I jumped! I looked to my left and this guy with this huge and handsome smile waived at me and kept walking. So I put down my food and jumped out of my car and screamed, "Hey! Don't be sneaking up on people like that are you crazy? Do I even know you?!"

So the guy came back to my car and introduced himself, still smiling, and asked me to get out of my car again so that he could take a look at me. I did just that because unfortunately I really didn't have much fear in me at that time. We began to talk and there was something about his charm that sucked me in real quick. We exchanged numbers and I promised I would call him. Later that week I fell into one of my never ending lonely states and called him. That day we decided we would hook up later after I had gotten off work. I remember telling him that I smoked weed and I didn't have time to fool around with anyone who didn't indulge. He laughed and said if I brought the cigars he would supply the weed. All of a sudden I really wanted to go see him.

When I walked into the apartment where he was staying he looked at me somewhat pitiful. For some reason that didn't bother me because I was trying to figure out if I thought he was fine instead of trying to see if he had good sense. So we hung out and got high and I spent the night. It had been a while since I had sex so I thought why not. That started a journey that was a real trip. It amazes me how people blame men for some things they should not. For example, when they see a woman with a truly promising future hook up with a man and then that woman's life turns to hell everyone blames the man. Saying things like, "Boy when she got with that man everything got terrible in her life." Everything was already getting terrible in my life. I had not even registered for school that fall. I thought why should I? I am not making good grades, I don't go to class, and the school has never been my thing. I always felt stupid anyway. I never really made good grades consistently even in high school.

So he and I became an item. For the first time, I had a boyfriend that would go places with me like 'my man.' He came with me to my friend's houses when we were hanging out and having sessions. He came with me to studios to work on music. It was like I had a man who was my best friend. I had no idea he was hanging with me to conquer me or leech off of me. I never considered such a thing. Remember what I said earlier about confessing extremes will cause you to do just the opposite and you will end up where you didn't want to be anyway? Well, that's exactly where I was headed. I thought I was very special to this man because of how much time we spent together. He never went to any of his classes either. I really didn't care because I was more concerned about finally having a friend by my side and a man by my side. Someone to understand me was more important that any goals or dreams. That friend should be Jesus dear sisters.

He didn't have his own place when I met him but he had a chance to become roommates with this girl he met. I never questioned how he met her. I just trusted it was innocent because I had roomed with a guy before and we never had sex or had any relationship whatsoever. I should have known she had gotten stung by disappointment by the way she looked at me when she first saw me. She pretended like she was happy to meet me. For some reason that made me feel good to know that I had him and she didn't. Mercy. Anyway, I ended almost living with him because my lights were off at my place and since he was constantly at my place before he got his own place, I figured he didn't mind. He began to complain about all my stuff finding its way to his place. By this time, I was so nervous because I know I didn't have the money I needed to get caught up on my bills. I was behind in everything. If it had not been for me having a job at a restaurant I would have starved.

One night, while I was doing his roommate's hair there, came a knock at the door. It was a female coming to see him. She looked at me like I was crazy and I had an awful feeling in the pit of my stomach. I invited her in and went to get my man. He pulled me into the room and said he just wanted to spend some time talking to her by himself for a while because she had been going through some stuff. I agreed. Although slightly I thought something was not quite right with that I didn't say anything and went back to doing hair. Then the roommate said, "Vawn, there is no way I would let my man be behind closed doors with another woman if I was you. That is crazy." I finished doing her hair and left.

I think about three days went by and I hadn't talked to my man. I was at one of my home boy's house recording some music when the same girl popped up at his house. She asked me to come outside to talk to me. This chick began to run down to me that my man had been trying to hook up with her before I came into the picture and basically that she wanted to be with him. But when she saw me, she decided to tell my man that he should be with me because she could tell that I was in love with him. I had just a little bit of self-respect left in me at that time and I was furious. I went looking for that Negro. I couldn't find him so I went to my girlfriend's house instead. I just decided to spend the night. I remember praying to God and saying, "If this man is for me then he will find me and apologize and never let it happen again." If you are not walking a righteous life and giving God the glory be careful who you think you are praying to. If you regard iniquity in your heart God will not hear you. (Psalm 66:18 and Isaiah 59:2 King James Version). The devil loves to try to play 'god' and seemingly bless you.

That morning about six o'clock, there came a knock at the door. It was him of course and he asked me to come outside to talk. I think it had been only 2 months into our relationship and already the drama had begun. He apologized and said that he would never allow another woman to come between us. He told me he loved me and that he wanted to be with me and could not imagine being with anyone else. I ate that up like filet mignon from a five-star restaurant. I hugged and kissed him and told God thank you because I knew he just had to be mine. Make no mistake about it; I had not given my life to Jehovah so the god I was thanking was satan. If you haven't made Jesus your Savior and Lord you are talking to your lord satan.

Ok, let's take a break from the story so that I can break down a few things. Honey, don't you ever let a man tell you he is not going to do something again when he has already done it right in your face! Are you hearing me? You better listen. God gives you plenty of clues on making the right decisions if you will listen to Him. I should have slammed that door in his face and told him to keep on stepping. You don't owe any man, anything, ever! Unless this man has told you he wants to marry you, put the ring on your figure, told your pastors and parents he wants to make you his wife, and you are in marriage counseling; baby, you don't owe him anything! Nothing! I hope you are hearing me. Don't tell me he has bought you tires for your car, paid your rent, bought your children school clothes, or taught your son how to use the bathroom upright. I really don't care. There is one, only one man, you owe your everything to. That man is Jesus and Jesus alone. When a man who says he loves you and wants to be in your life is ordained by God you will not have to make these kinds of decisions anyway. There will be NO drama. Sure there will be character developments that both of you will have to travel through for the purpose of coming together as one. But that is the only 'situations' you will have to deal with. That usually deals with you both dying to your selfish selves so that the kingdom of God can begin to shine through you and build your character for the glory of God the Father. Whew! I had to get that off of my chest real quick. Let's move on.

Money was so very tight between both of us. I did not go home for Christmas that year. I stayed with my man at his friend's apartment. It was cool being with someone that loved me. I thought this man was sent to me to love me and be my husband forever. We talked about being together for Christmas and how special that was for both of us. We were also concerned about paying bills and he told me that he was thinking about taking his gun and robbing some pizza delivery boys. I was shocked but obviously not shocked enough because that should have made me run away from him. I was so worried about him so we talked about stupid ideas that could be considered just as dangerous.

By this time I was completely co-dependent on him and could not stand to be without him for even a second. He became my new addiction. So one night we went to pull off the act. I was telling him the whole way maybe we really should not do this because we could get into a lot of trouble. He told me I was just being scary and nothing would happen so be quiet about it. So we got to the building and he broke in through the window. I told him I wanted to go home and he told me to be quiet and let's get this done. I didn't want to lose my man and I didn't want to get in trouble. I didn't want to go back to being all alone again. I tell you if God ever allows me to gain true financial freedom I will sew a huge seed that place school that was defiled by my momentary retardation. I should have gotten my keys and took off running back to my car. Instead, I started crying and pleaded with him to leave. He fussed at me about being scary and about punking out on him. What was I to do? He was my man and I loved him. So thank God we left.

The ride home was terrible. It was as if I had let my man down and he was no longer in love with me. I wanted to make him proud of me but I didn't want this criminal life. I had my brush with it a few years before and I had learned my lesson. All I wanted now was for us to become married and be happy forever. I may as well been smoking crack because that is exactly what that thought sounds like. When we got back to the apartment he wouldn't stay in the same room with me. I tried to talk to him but he ignored me so much. I rolled a blunt and asked him if he wanted to smoke it with me. No weed head will turn down a fresh optimal blunt. So that was my way of keeping him close to me at that point. I tried my best to stay up all night with him. Something in me was still so scared and nervous. I thought about hiding my keys but I decided that I was being crazy. So I lay down to sleep because I was too high and sleepy to stay up.

I woke up about 7 am. My man was not in the apartment and neither were my keys. I ran outside to see if my car was outside and it wasn't. I really cannot describe to you the feeling I had inside of me. It was so much fear and so much confusion. At this point in my life, my name was Vawn Confusion Stearnes. About an hour after I woke my man came back home. I ran to him and I was relieved. That stingy man had smoked up all the rest of the weed while I was asleep so I couldn't get high. You ever ask a question knowing you know the answer anyway? But you ask it because you hope that somehow the answer will change. So I asked him, "Where were you?" Let me take one more break just in case you missed something important. I should have called the cops and told them that this man stole my keys and took my car without my permission. I should have gone off on him for taking my car without my freaking permission. But see I had let him take my car and do whatever he wanted just to keep him happy so he didn't think he had to ask me. Sisters, you always know the answer before you ask it. But I understand why we ask. It is almost to confirm ourselves. If we are honest with ourselves most of the time we really don't want to hear the truth anyway.

He was smoking a cigarette when he answered, "I was just out riding because I had to clear my head." I was happy to hear that lie so I gave him a hug and told him I was worried about him and asked him to never leave without telling me. He told a lie to me again and assured me he would never do that again. I was staying with him mostly still at this time because I had not gotten my electricity restored so I never really went to my apartment but to feed my cat. About 3 days after this happened I went to feed my cat. I walked in and there was equipment from the music department all over my apartment. I almost peed on myself. I'm serious too because I stood there blinking my eyes thinking somehow what was in front of me would change. Sike! It was real alright.

I drove about 100 mph back to his trailer to question him. His response to me was to be quiet because he knew what he was doing and we both needed money so I should be happy because he was going to share it with me. I just stood there in disbelief. He decided to take some of the equipment to his place because he was going to sell some of it and wanted easy access to it. His roommate, being as nosey as any woman who wanted a man and didn't really get him, decided to go through his room one day when we were not there. My man told me he had to tell her everything to shut her up and promised her some of the goods. Well, somehow he pissed her off really bad. I remember this like it was yesterday.

    I woke up a cold morning in the country. I looked outside without getting up fully. The sun was not out and it looked so gloomy. The wind was blowing and the little fragile trees trying to grow through the winter were busy dancing in the wind. All of a sudden there was pounding at the door. Hard knocking like the person who was knocking had brass knuckles. My heart quickly climbed up to my throat and took residence out of place. We jumped up and he said to get the weed and flush it down the toilet! I stood there like a deer caught in lights. He screamed at me again. I grabbed the weed and called myself hiding it in the medicine cabinet because I wanted my weed. I really didn't know what was happening. But the accomplished criminal that he knew exactly what was happening. I thank God for this man for two very good reasons, which will learn about later, but the truth is still the truth.

    Detectives and police flooded the little trailer. His roommate was outside with one of the detectives. They came in with an arrest warrant and told me to sit my butt down and don't move. I did sit down shaking like crazy. My skin was tightening on me and my stomach was ill. They found the weed and came out of the room and handcuffed my man. He said I told you to flush it! I said nothing. I just looked like a scared naïve suburban girl completely out of her element. You know what flashed through my head at that moment? Thoughts of me performing in my high school plays and performing in the band playing my flute so beautifully. I thought about being in the brownies, then girl scouts, and then 4-H. I thought about performing in the NAACP black history performance and becoming the Youth Correspondence Secretary for the State of Texas. I thought about performing in my high school choir and how much fun and joy that brought to my life. I thought about winning the economics scholarship. I thought about band camp and marching. I thought about all of the performances I had so well accomplished at the University. I thought about the choir performances I had achieved. I thought about my sorority and pledging. I thought about how many people, including myself, saw me as a person who would be a success. I wondered how I could go from so much opportunity to this. I figured perhaps I deserved all of this. This man was my only family because my real family was torn apart so who cares? However, at that moment my thoughts came back to the reality that I was on my way to utter failure. I knew my man would leave me because I didn't flush the weed down the toilet. I wanted to kick his roommate's butt for being so spiteful and telling. I thought life was pretty hopeless at this point.

He went to jail and they took me to the interrogation room. I sang like a bird because I was so scared. They took me to my apartment and got all of the stolen goods. I remember one of the detectives found my weed box. It had remnants of weed bits in it. He asked me was it mine and I told him to his face, "no." He smiled at me and said, "Ok no problem." So they let me go and I went to my girlfriends' house. I ended up going to see my man in jail and he told me about a man that could help him get out of jail. The total value of all that he stole was over $25,000. I helped him get out of jail for the next week. I was visiting him every day and calling that man every day.

Finally, the man called me and said he would be out that afternoon. This was about a week and a half later. I was so happy. Now the friends he had whose apartment we spent time at decided to throw him a 'getting out of jail party.' This is good so I hope you are paying attention to how stupid I was. I was no longer naïve and ignorant. I was downright stupid in love and depressed and in a confused state of being. I was waiting at the apartment with everyone. When my man called they put me on the phone and he said he wasn't able to get out right then. So I left crying my eyes out in front of everyone. I went back to my girlfriend's house and called the man that helped him get out. He said to me that he was out and he should be home now. I was like what!

So I went back to the apartment and don't you know that Negro was in that apartment. I felt like such a used and stupid creature. Here I am spending my days and nights on your behind and you not only embarrass me but do me like this. I questioned him in front of everyone. He smoothed talked me quiet. He said he was mad at me for telling him. If I had kept my mouth shut he would not have been in trouble. I said, "You had all that stuff (I really used another word) in my apartment and I didn't steal that stuff. I would have gone to jail!" He was like I know but I thought you loved me and real love doesn't tell. Real love doesn't tell. Jesus.

We ended up going to a party that night and I felt so uncomfortable and alone anyway. My friends ended up pretty much leaving me alone and it was only my man and me. One day, while we were sleeping at my apartment there, came a knock on the door and the constable was on the other side. My apartment management had filed eviction on me and said I had to be out by the weekend. I packed up all that I could muster and we moved to Texas. I really have to take a cry break.

Dear Sis,

Number 1- Never let the love of a mere man pull you away from what you are supposed to be doing with your life. Your call and your God given purpose. I can't really say that I wish I never met him because we eventually had two children together. Remember I said I have two good reasons to thank God for him? Well, they are the two. Man our children are beautiful and awesome. They are so smart and intelligent a just perfect. Well to me anyway. Smile.

What I know now is I should not have responded to him when he knocked on my window that night. I should not have cared that he was in jail. I should have packed my things and went back to my mother in Texas alone. But I didn't. Like I said I really don't want to erase this because my babies are here.

All I can say to you sisters is this is clearly a terrible relationship. This man did not love me. He was truly out for what best fit him and him alone. I am not saying that he purposed to be this horrible to me. I think he really wanted to be a good person. We are all lost apart from the righteous foundation of the Holy Spirit sisters. That is the bottom line. Without Jesus, nothing in life will work completely for you. I know that God allowed this to happen in my life and I trust Him for that.

I know that I gave up on myself at that time because I thought no one loved me. Jesus loved me even then and there was still protection on my life even in the midst of all of that turmoil. And all of that turmoil had truly just begun. I know that if I would have really attached myself to Jesus, His loved would have caused me to see the reality of what I was in and I would have avoided so much heartache and pain. But thank you Jesus that God is the God of another chance! Halleluiah!

Jeremiah 29:11 King James

For I know the thoughts that I think toward you, saith the Lord, thoughts of peace, and not of evil, to give you an expected end.

Chapter 7 – Almost Dead

I thank God that I lived through so much of these times I am sharing. I and my man moved to Texas with all that we could fit into my two-door car. It was stuffed. I remember being stopped by the police as we were just entering into Texas. My man had me put our weed stash into my bra while the two officers searched my car. I would have never gotten stopped if I was by myself. All of the many times I traveled to Texas in that very car and now I am getting stopped. They searched the car slowly and it truly aggravated me. They let us go and we were on my way. I had already made plans to move in with a friend of mine from my home town.

That was a really dumb decision. Anyway, we moved in with her and she, in turn, developed a crush on my man. I remember one day I was about to move and leave his behind with her and this guy we all knew came to smoke with me. He explained to me that he wishes he would have just dealt with some of his ex-girlfriend's issues and stayed with her. He explained how much hurt he was going through as a result of leaving her and would not want anyone to deal with it. Let's take a break.

Don't be so ready to avoid hurt. Sometimes hurting can cause you to grow up real fast, get stronger and begin to make sound choices. So when my man came home he noticed my car packed and it messed with him enough to act right for at least 2 more weeks! I decided to get our own place. Did you see that? I decided. That is upside down. A man is supposed to be the leader in a relationship. Let's talk about that for a minute. If you are the type of woman who has to control everything I need you to get down on your knees right now and ask the Lord to remove that spirit of control off of your life. It is in perfect order for a man to lead. This is how God the Father ordained a household to operate. (Ephesians 5:21-33)

After we got our own place things between us were about the same really. He still went to visit this girl and her family. I remember I was complaining about that to my mother and she said, "Well what do you expect, you are the one that brought him to them." I couldn't do anything but swallow that medicine. I did, however, go with one of my co-workers to a party. Our plan was to go to this house party and then go to a local club. At the house party my man came a brought me this girl who was telling him about some pills. She said that taking one of these very small pills was like smoking two blunts. I took one of the pills and broke it half. When I did that it crumbled into about 3 crazy pieces. I was nervous about taking the pill but I did anyway. I swallowed one of the small pieces thinking that was a safer choice. I think I really didn't have any love for myself anymore. My self-worth was completely attached to this man that didn't have any self-worth himself, bless his heart.

We all went to the club and I had a drink I believe. That night is really a blur. I remember dancing and beginning to get so sleepy. I told everyone that I would wait in the car for them because I was sleepy. My man let me go to my car to sleep, high and at nighttime at a club. But I loved him so very much. Let's break. The bible says to a husband that he should love his wife as Christ loved the church. Christ died for the church, protected the church, lived for the church, built up the church, caused the church to experience progressive and positive change, and Christ loved the church with all of his being. Allowing a woman to sleep in car, knowing she is loaded out of her mind, is clearly none of what I just described. Allowing her to get zooted out of her mind in the first place is an issue. I hope that is crystal clear.

Anything could have happened to me. Lord Jesus I give you glory right now for protecting me. I remember knocking woke me up out of my addicted stupor. My man and my co-worker were knocking like crazy on my widow. I looked at them like they were crazy. When I opened the door I said, "What's wrong with you guys, you could have broken my window!" They then explained to me that they were getting ready to call the ambulance because they had been knocking for about 5 minutes. God, and God alone woke me up because I could have been dead and woke up in hell. Lord Jesus.

Later that week I noticed bruises beginning to form on my body. I did not have insurance at the time so I didn't go to the doctor. I remember people thinking my man had begun beating on me. I told them they were crazy because I would never let a man treat me crazy and abuse me. One of the bruises was so big that my mother saw it and decided to have me go to her doctor. The doctor sent me away to take a series of blood tests. I was told that the following week my results would be in and they would contact me. Two days later I came into my job from lunch and saw my mother standing in my boss's office. I froze because my mother has never come to any of my jobs and the look on my boss's face looked like she had seen a ghost.

I walked in and they both looked at me for a second before talking and then put on the fakest smile they both could muster up. My mother explained that the doctor had called her and said that more tests were needed and she needed to pick me up and take me to the hospital. My boss came around her desk and hugged me as if to say goodbye. I was obviously nervous. Honestly, I was not even thinking about smoking weed at that moment. My mother and I got into her car and I asked her to explain to me what was going on. She said, "Well the doctor called me and said that the tests revealed a big problem that we needed to look at. You really need to stay calm because getting excited could cause you harm. The doctor said that if we would have waited until next week you could have di…" I cut her off, "Died!!" She rolled her eyes as if to be mad at herself for going that far.

I calmed down real quick and I told her I loved her a lot for picking me up. I just knew I was about to die for real. I had always prayed that I would know when I was about to die so that I could say goodbye to people. We took the 30 minute drive to Galveston, Texas. We were headed for UTMB hospital which still has one of the top hematology labs in Texas. It was such a very beautiful spring day. The sky was perfectly blue and there were a few dusty clouds playing in the sky. On the way to Galveston there are such awesome beach houses to see gathered together along the highway. I started to think about when I was a little girl and how many times we drove along this same path to visit my grandmother or go to eat at my favorite Chinese restaurant. We would go to church on Sundays when all four of us would actually go to church together. My mother always made me go to church with her even if my Dad and brother would not go. Thank God for that push.

We got to the hospital emergency room and there were tones of people. I was really glad about that because that meant that I would face the inevitable later. We were in the hospital for about 10 minutes when I looked up and saw my dad. I was so scared at that moment. I was thinking, "What is he doing here? He came and gave me a hug and asked how I was doing. I told him I didn't know. All of a sudden someone called my name to be seen. I was there for 15 minutes only and behind all of these other people and they called me in. I was now terrified. As ignorant as I was back then I knew getting called in fast meant there was an extreme emergency and I didn't even know what was wrong with me.

The doctor came in with that same forced smile that my mother and boss had and asked me how I was doing. I told her I would be doing much better if I knew what was going on with me. She said she had to put me through a few tests to fully answer that question accurately. I agreed. I took a cat scan, more blood work, and a whole host of test on big machines that frighten the heck out of me. When I got back to the room my parents were still there and it was so beautiful to see them sitting by each other so calm and pleasant. I had not seen that in years and years and years. In the middle of all of that chaos, I found happiness in that picture and stored it in my memory.

The doctor came back with all of her knowledge and explained to me that I had a disease called ITP or Idiopathic thrombocytopenic purpura. This is the condition of having a low platelet count of no known cause. Most causes appear to be related to antibodies that are developed those attack platelets. ITP can be a disease that is asymptomatic which means a patient can carry a disease or infection but experience no symptoms; however, a very low platelet count can lead to visible symptoms such as purpura (bruises) or more seriously, bleeding diathesis. Bleeding diathesis is an unusual susceptibility to bleeding mostly due to a defect in the system of coagulation. Several types are distinguished, ranging from mild to lethal. The body is supposed to have between 150,000 and 250,000 platelets in the body at any given time. I had 700 in my body at the time. It was explained to me that I really should have been dead and they were surprised that I walked into the hospital alive. They had already prepared my parents with counseling for the possibility of me dying while I was taking tests. No one expected me to live.

After she explained this to me, I really had no words except, "So basically I am dying." She put on that same fake and forced smile and said, "Well, that was something they were going to try to prevent." Try. She then told me to let anyone know if I had a headache. I told her I have one now. She asked if I had eaten anything and I told her I had not so she ordered a sandwich for me. I asked why it was such a big deal if I had a headache and she said that it could be a result of hemorrhaging in the brain. I don't guess I have to tell you that really took me to a place of total fear. The doctor said that I will be admitted to the hospital for at least a week and after that week we will determine whether or not I should stay.

When I got to the room the hospital staff made sure I was comfortable and stable. I was visited by many doctors and students of the hospital. UTMB is also a school for medical professionals. I had to explain that I did take a pill that I didn't know what it was or the name, that I smoked cigarettes, drank liquor and smoked weed heavily. My parents were asked to leave the room when we talked about that thank God. They seemed not be so much worried about the weed as they were about the cigarettes and that mystery pill. I was told the disease had been lying dormant in me and the chemical imbalance of that pill and the cigarettes triggered the disease to flare up. I was told to immediately stop smoking cigarettes and never take that pill again. I promised I would and I did stop smoking cigarettes. Let's break. Please don't wait until there is an active gun against your head to get your health in order. Stop smoking cigarettes and indulging in drugs they will kill you quickly. Look at it this way. If you are on top of a 55 story office building and decide to jump off – if half way down you are not dead yet, are you still in a good position? Nope!

I asked my mom if my man had contacted her and she said he had and she told him about everything that was going on. He told her that he would come and spend the night with me at the hospital. He did not show up at all. I spent that night by myself. I know now that I was not by myself and that the Holy Spirit was there protecting me. I did pray. I asked God to forgive me for all of the mess I had allowed myself to get into. I asked God to show me if this man really loved me as if He had not already been showing me. I told God that if I closed my eyes and they did not open in the morning to please allow me to awake with Him heaven.

The next morning a priest came by to visit with me and pour holy water on me and prayed for me. Then a nice lady who was an evangelist of the hospital prayed with me. After taking more tests and trying a medicine called prednisone, my platelets began to increase in number. This was a very good thing because if the medicine did not work they would have to do surgery and/or a blood transfusion. It would just turn into a big mess. Because my platelet count had started to rise slowly they decided I could go home. Go home? Yes somehow God decided I was worthy enough to live. Thank God for the purpose of my life because

I am still here. I went home and every week for 10 months I week to get tested at the hospital and check my platelet count. Every week they rose higher and higher until I was again stable. God blessed me with healing and life and glory to God for that! The disease has never again re-surfaced. I was taking 100mg of that medicine a day for 3 months. This medicine is a steroid so I gained all that weight back plus some in ten months. But thank you, Jesus, I was healed. I did not stop smoking weed.

My man had not made it to the hospital. I asked him what happened and he said that he had eventually come to the hospital that night and he was not allowed up the room at night. I asked him why he didn't wait until morning and meet me back at the hospital. No answer. I was at my mother's apartment when he finally showed up. I was actually mad at him for real but still didn't leave this man. Even after God had saved me from death, I had not attached myself to His love. I didn't know what God's love was back then. I had no idea that God's love covers and protects you. I went back to my apartment with my man and back to depression.

Dear Sis,

I love my former husband for loving me long enough to produce such beautiful children. Yet, I know that I should have left him alone that day. When I heard this man say he was cool with leaving me in the hospital and I was almost dead that should have said something to me. God is constantly giving us clues on what to do and what not to do. God told me once to use my common God sense. Meaning, there are just some things that are dumb and we know it. We just choose not to know it. God made us perfectly.

I know that my parents really loved me but I still didn't see it for the simple reason I could not see love because I did not know what love was. If you do not know God's love, you have not known real love. I know that I will forever give God the glory for saving me that day. We all have a purpose here in this life and you have to ask God what His purpose is for you in your life. I know that He will show you if you don't know at this time. If you know what that purpose is then to get busy doing God's work. If you are a radio DJ perhaps your purpose is to bring hope in the words you choose over the airwaves. If you are a teacher or professor perhaps your purpose is to guide your students into their purpose.

Purpose does not have to be a defined ministry in the church. Ministry is using what God has created for you to do and to glorify the Kingdom of God. I did not do that. I stayed in the same mess I was in before God healed me. I know that God started truly calling on me then and in the years that would follow, I would answer. But first He had to allow me to sink a bit deeper in order to get my attention. It is a scary place when you know there is a God and still you reject Him.

Romans 1:18-37 NIV

The wrath of God is being revealed from heaven against all the godlessness and wickedness of men who suppress the truth by their wickedness since what may be known about God is plain to them, because God has made it plain to them. For since the creation of the world God's invisible qualities—his eternal power and divine nature—have been clearly seen, being understood from what has been made, so that men are without excuse.

For although they knew God, they neither glorified him as God nor gave thanks to him, but their thinking became futile and their foolish hearts were darkened. Although they claimed to be wise, they became fools and exchanged the glory of the immortal God for images made to look like mortal man and birds and animals and reptiles.

Therefore God gave them over in the sinful desires of their hearts to sexual impurity for the degrading of their bodies with one another. They exchanged the truth of God for a lie and worshiped and served created things rather than the Creator—who is forever praised. Amen.

Because of this, God gave them over to shameful lusts. Even their women exchanged natural relations for unnatural ones. In the same way, the men also abandoned natural relations with women and were inflamed with lust for one another. Men committed indecent acts with other men and received in themselves the due penalty for their perversion.

Furthermore, since they did not think it worthwhile to retain the knowledge of God, he gave them over to a depraved mind, to do what ought not to be done. They have become filled with every kind of wickedness, evil, greed and depravity. They are full of envy, murder, strife, deceit and malice. They are gossips, slanderers, God-haters, insolent, arrogant and boastful; they invent ways of doing evil; they disobey their parents; they are senseless, faithless, heartless and ruthless. **Although they know God's righteous decree that those who do such things deserve death, they not only continue to do these very things but also approve of those who practice them.**

Chapter 8 – Trying to Get Back to Me

I had a chance to play keyboard for a local band and I jumped at the chance. I figured here was my chance to get back into the game of music again. I needed something to make me smile because a friend of mine had gone to pick up my man from one of his other girlfriend's house and I was so embarrassed but I stayed with him anyway. It was February of 1999 and I was just as lonely in love with this man as ever. The band was a great release. The music we played sucked big-time but I played with them anyway because I was at least trying to get back to myself. Now here is the deal. When you are involved in anything that keeps you from doing what you love and your natural purpose, then you need to wake up and get out. For as long as I can remember I was doing something in music and the arts. But as soon as I got in this relationship, I could not seem to get involved in what I really loved which is music and the arts. That is a really big point. Would God give you talents and desires and expect you not to use them? Let's move on.

We had the opportunity to play at a club and I was to sing a song while playing keys. I remember while performing my song I looked up and my man was at the bar and a lady approached my man. I was actually having a great set because my voice was on the pitch and I could feel that my delivery was excellent. I was singing about love and relationship and the balance in understanding one another and trust. I guess somehow I was beginning to allow myself to feel challenged to make the relationship work myself. I began to convince myself that if I truly had his back the other women would go away. I don't know why I was not sharp enough to understand that he was the one going for the women. You can never change a man. You can never wait for a man to become and the man of God or think that your walk with Christ will influence good behavior or godly behavior from a man. God really doesn't need your help in encouraging a man to walk uprightly.

Anyway while singing a great set I looked and saw this woman talking to my man. I noticed her purposely talking to him in a way that would make him move closer to her and he did just that. In a matter of seconds, her breasts were pressed up against him while they were talking in each other's ears. Right in front of me! I wanted to come down off of the stage and let the beast in me roar! But I didn't because I am a professional. After the set, I walked up to both of them and stood in between them and 'made my presence known'. Listen, my sisters, this is not necessary. If this man is from God he would back up and make his love known. Halleluiah! Can you hear me?

The lady backed up like one inch almost as if to say, "I was here first." God is just dropping this one me. He most likely was telling her something that made her think she had a chance with him. I am sure he didn't know how long my set was going to be so I am sure he thought he had time to get his 'mack on' interrupted. So I introduced myself because he didn't bother. She said, "Oh I didn't know ok girlfriend it's cool." Then I went back on stage to do another set and she kept her distance. My man, of course, talked to me like I was crazy saying that I did not have to do that because I make people feel uncomfortable around me. That really encouraged fear, self-doubt, and insecurity in me. When the set was over we were finished for the night. I went to say hi to a few people who were congratulating me on my excellent singing. There was a huge mirror on the entire wall. While I was bending over talking to someone that was sitting down, I saw that same lady approach my man from a little distance and hold up her thumb and pinky as if to say 'call me.'

Was I crunk?! Was I hot under the collar? Oh yes, honey, the boldness was bursting out then. So I ran up on my man and said, "What the heck are you doing? You just have to disrespect me huh? Well, I am going to show you what happens when you do that in my face!" I am laughing at myself right now, although this was clearly not a laughing matter. I just can't believe I didn't pick up a bar stool and climb upside his head with it! I'm just kidding. Honestly not really but I must say that violence is not the key. My point is he is the problem NOT that lady. I ran after this woman and found her in the ladies room. I confronted her and I asked her, "Why did you do that?"

She said, "Did what," like I am stupid or something. I explained to her that I saw her in the mirror tell my man to call her. I asked her what kind of woman would still pursue a man and his woman was right there making her presence known. I was really ready to fight. She started to apologize and say that if she was me she would be doing the same thing. She said she had a 15-year-old daughter at home and she understood how young people think. I told her she should go home and be with her instead of being 45 and chasing a 28-year-old man. She kept saying that she was sorry and I didn't have to worry about her trying to get involved with him. It caused a scene. My man came out right after she walked away. He said he couldn't believe my behavior and said he would find his own way home. So I went back into the club and sat at the bar to get loaded. I sat there with a couple of boyfriends and we enjoyed music and sang together. I left at about 2 am. My car had a flat tire. I couldn't get the stupid tire off. I drove it flat for about 5 miles until I got close to my Dad's apartment and luckily he answered the phone and met me where I was to change it for me. I supposed I looked so disgusted he didn't ask any questions. A man that loves you is supposed to cover you.

****

After that he decided he would move back to his home town which was in another state. I was devastated. I received that the problems in our relationship was my fault. By that time a friend of mine from college had come to Houston to live with me and start her life there. She had met someone and I saw her boyfriend all the time. I was unable to handle not being with a man. After all, this man was my family being that I thought I had no one. I remember one day my friend was noticing how sad I was and she said if you still love him then maybe you owe it to yourself to see if you could make it work. She said that she had been through that pain before and she would hate for anyone to go through it. So I decided I would go to his home town to pick him up and bring him back.

Let us break for a minute. Get you some good godly friends. I am talking about sisters who will tell you the God truth about yourself. Not help you stay in the same miserable state of mind and supporting your bad decisions. We need someone around us who will not cackle and agree with mess in our lives but encourage us to head straight for Jesus. That is plain and as simple as it gets. Please take heed to that. Also your friends must have a heart for the betterment of your successful welfare and not be envious or jealous of God taking to success.

I really didn't even know my way around that city that well. It was hard calling him because his mother didn't really like me. He had convinced her that it was my entire fault that he got in trouble with the law. Let's not even consider the fact that somehow she must have forgotten that before he met me he had been consistently in trouble with the law every year since he was about 10 years old! There is always someone to perpetuate and support bad behavior. Parents must hold their children accountable for their wrong choices; otherwise, the court system will do it for them. When I arrived 6 hours later from Houston, I went to the front door and knocked on it. Thanks be to God it was a really beautiful day outside. She opened the door and looked at me through the barred screen door and said, "What do you want?"

No kidding. She knew who I was because I had been there several times with him. I am sure he told her terrible things about me because that is how he got someone to feel sorry for him. He would tell all of the awful things that were being done to him and cry about it like he was so sensitive and pathetic; and, I ate that mess up every time he fed it to me. She didn't say come in I know you have been driving a long time. She could have just said hello to me. She was so mean about it but I am not mad at her because she was treating me based on what she thought I was doing to her 'little boy.' I told her he called me and asked me to come and get him. She looked shocked. So in the 'hood', the straight up 'hood', she closed the door and left me outside to go and get him. When he came to the door he unlocked the door and let me in.

While I stayed there overnight his mother confronted me and said if you love him so much why don't you marry him. I explained that I wasn't ready for that. She said well you are living in sin and if we really loved each other that much then we should get married. She didn't know but that really convicted me. I wasn't walking with the Lord but I did know who Jesus was and I claimed to be a Christian. This was the fall of 1999. My man and I traveled back to Houston. He didn't have a job and that was not unusual. I had confidence in him that he would get a job though because it seemed like he didn't mind working.

When we got back to Houston we had a conversation about getting married. It was mostly my conversation. We did get married with the justice of the peace. It was a small, simple and cute little ceremony. We did it so fast that his parents were not able to make it. Honestly, I didn't care because I thought she hated me anyway because that is the way his mother treated me. I didn't even feel comfortable making love to him that night because my heart was so hurt. I knew that I had made a mistake but I was hoping for the best. I really loved this man.

He was my everything. That right there is a problem. Even if a man is sent from God, God should continue to be your everything. The one and only something that will never change is God and God alone.

    Four months later one morning I got up and said good morning to my Dad. He had been staying with us for a spell. The phone rang and it was a sweet little female voice saying, "Yeah can I speak to…" She was asking for my man. Now he had been doing a little electrician work, so he said. So I figured that was the purpose for her call. I said, "Well he is not in can I take a message or is there some work you need to check on." She plainly told me, "Sure you can tell him Tracey called and this is a personal call." I realized she said it that way for a purpose. I got her number and I told her I would make sure he would call her later. I was so embarrassed because my Dad was there and he heard the whole thing. His advice to me was to think about how I had been treating him to make sure that I am giving him everything he needs because if I am not that will make a man cheat on you. I am not mad at my Father for that advice. However, a man of God, married not dating, will provoke you to naturally nurture and care for him. If you go through something yourself he will keep himself while praying for you. I can give you a list of men of God that I know would do the same. But here is the deal, I was giving that man ALL that I had so he had no excuse. That was not the best advice. Bless family but unless someone is leading you to the truth of Christ, get them out of your ear now!

    When he got home he told me he had met one of his mother's cousins and she would be calling him. I asked him where he had met her and he said at work. I explained that she called him that morning and I did that while dialing her phone number. When she answered I told her to hold on to him and told him to come to the phone because I had his cousin on the phone. Of course, he didn't get on the phone. We broke up that night for about a day. He came back and promised he would get it together. I took him back and believe him and I considered it was partly my fault because I married him without trusting him. That is such bull. I told myself that I would leave him if it happened one more time. One week later I took a pregnancy test and my beautiful daughter was coming. Now I had to make my marriage work.

Dear Sis,

I promised that I would keep it real with you on this journey. I supposed that the reason why I cry at the end of each chapter is I sit here and ask myself how I let myself go through all of this. I know that God did heal me of the hurt and pain from the past. Honestly, I know now that God is ministering to me right now because I need to not ask myself that anymore and I have truly received God's forgiveness for my choices.

I know that I should have gotten that marriage annulled. I know that I was so co-dependent on this man that it was killing me. Fortunately, I had stopped smoking weed a month before I got pregnant because I was nervous that I would get pregnant and I didn't want to expose my baby to that mess. God does hate divorce but that relationship was not of God. I was still bound to the vows I took before God. This is a touchy subject so let us apply the word. God will only release you from your vows if there is adultery involved. At the same time you still have the option to forgive and I would encourage anyone to forgive their husband or wife and try to do their best to make it work. You should never give up on your marriage and never give up on giving God the change to make your marriage work. The only way a marriage works is if both parties will give themselves to God. However, people go years waiting for one spouse to come to God and they have to wait if that is God's will.

I was the one who said that I was going to be loyal to my vows and stick it out because I knew that my husband would stop cheating on me. I don't know why I lied to myself like that because he was cheating on me before I married him. At any rate, I wanted to give God a chance to fix my husband. So I stayed with him. There is absolutely nothing wrong with that. This is called courage and having faith in God. But if your mate doesn't change and stays in adultery I would encourage you to seek God and godly counsel (your Pastor) on what do as far as staying in the marriage or leaving. Only God can tell you to leave a marriage based on his word. Here again you can always forgive.

Because this is a ministry for women who are not married let me be clear. DO NOT MARRY A MAN THAT IS NOT A MAN OF GOD. DO NOT MARRY A MAN THAT ALREADY DISPLAYS CHARACTER THAT HURTS YOU, DEPRESSES YOU, CONDEMNS YOU, AND ABUSES YOU! This is NOT of God. I hope that is clear. If you find that you are always holding your breath in hopes that you will not be disappointed then there is one of two things at work. Either you need counseling and need to be healed from past hurts because you are walking in fear or the man you are with did not come from God. (Please note that I do not want you to say to yourself the reason why I am hurt all the time is because of 'Me'. Even if you are the problem and the man comes from God, he will love you enough to get you into counseling.) With God, there are no disappointments. Let me be clear. There will be room to build your character, but no hurtful disappointments. We will discover that more in later chapters.

Revelation 7:17 amplified

For the Lamb Who is in the midst of the throne will be their Shepherd, and He will guide them to the springs of the waters of life; and God will wipe away every tear from their eyes.

Chapter 9 – My First Born

Now I was pregnant and that was a great incentive to get my marriage on track. What track I'm not sure as I reflect right now, but on track nonetheless. I was working at a cell phone company and it was a really decent job. I hadn't gotten the CP time out of me just yet but I was there and I did a great job once I arrived. The ladies I worked with were the best. Even now I thank God for them. We all had our share of issues. I had the pleasure of seeing one of the ladies at Lakewood Church at a creative writing seminar years later, which was absolutely fabulous and was able to express my love for all they did for me. See when it was close to the time for me to have the baby I came to work one day and my desk was literally flooded with gifts. They gave me things I didn't even know that I needed. Because I had another baby right after that, those gifts became a bigger blessing to me as I used them for my son as well.

Right after we got married (maybe a month) my man had taken this guy to get some weed. Well, the guy actually was a street hustler so he sold weed. My man was taking him with the promise of some free weed. As much of a criminal as he was, I never had faith in him that he knew what he was doing. I am going to take you back for a minute. One evening, right before we got married I was on my way home to my apartment with my girlfriend. We were roommates at the time and her boyfriend lived there with us as well. I was walking to the apartment and this girl stopped me and said, "You man spent the night with me last night." Just like that and right in my face. My girlfriend almost choked. Not because she was shocked either, but she was hoping I didn't go ballistic on her. I asked her questions to confirm what she was saying. Obviously, I confronted my man about it and he convinced me that he was there because he was mad at me for "not understanding him." So he put the blame on me which made me want to love him more so that he could treat me better. I got that from my father being an alcoholic when I was little. I learned that in 2006 and we will talk about that later. Just so that we can be clear right here let me explain a little.

When you have an alcoholic parent or a parent addicted to anything, they come home drunk and they really don't have time for you. Not because they don't love you necessary, but because they are drunk plain and simple. So the message you get is "I love you but not right now. I love you but go away right now." Then in the morning when they are somewhat sober they are ready to love on you because of their guilt. So you do things for them to make them feel better and they are ready to show their love now. This teaches you that if you love someone harder they will be ready to love you back. Again I say, sometimes the truth is not easy to digest but it is the truth anyway. Let's move on.

After my man explained to me that it was my fault that he spent the night with a woman that lived 3 doors down from us, (wow) is when he decided he would take the guy to get his new stash of weed. I told my man that I didn't think this was a good idea. He fussed at me and told me I was tripping. I had stopped smoking weed completely I was afraid I would get pregnant and I did not want a crack baby. He left and went anyway. There is something to be said about women's intuition. We are given discernment from God regarding our husbands. That night about 2 have I received a call from him telling me that right after he had dropped off the guy he had been stopped by the police. No duh right? The guy had stayed at the house and they wanted my man so that he could snitch on everyone in that house and ultimately bring down one of the billions of weed houses in the world. Anyway, he explained to me that while the cop was at his car he took off running. I screamed at him, "Where the freak is my car!" He explained to me that he left the car and the keys. Lord have mercy. He ran from a helicopter and hid in some bushes next to a house. Apparently, he found some crack head and promised him some weed if he would hide him.

My friend's man and I went to pick him up. Sure enough while just driving down the street as instructed the crack head came out into the street and stood in front of our moving vehicle and had us stop. He asked us if we were looking for someone. I told him, yes and my man ran out from somewhere and jumped in the car. My man paid the very happy crack head and we left. When I went to get my car I guess you know it was pure hell trying to get it back. I had no keys and nothing to prove it was mine. Lord Jesus. Please don't say love will make you do stupid things. 'Us' being stupid makes us do stupid things, ok? Let's move on.

He eventually had to turn himself in because they were looking for him obviously. I don't know what the heck is up with the criminal system because he was already on parole for the other crime but they gave him 2 weekends in jail for his crime. He would go in on Friday and come out on Sunday. Now let us move forward to my family reunion while I was pregnant.

The beauty of me being pregnant was my brother and I found out that we were pregnant at the same time; that is, his wife was pregnant. (I see you smiling) I remember calling him to tell him he was going to be an uncle and he said to me that I was going to be an aunt. I thought he was playing with me because I said yeah right. After a moment of silence, we realized we had found out the very same week. What a treat. My brother and I had a lot of issues growing up. He verbally abused me really bad and beat me up all the time. I remember begging my father not to go out to sell insurance and stay home to protect me. He never did of course because he had to go out and run his business. When I got out of the hospital in 1998 my brother had said something really ugly to me and I told him I wouldn't say that to my only sibling who almost died. That was the last time my brother said anything to me ugly ever again in my life. Now that we were pregnant at the same time this was a chance to get closer and that did happen over time. We hug and kiss all the time now. In 2004 I invited him to church. I know I am out of order chronologically right now but I am lead to go here now. My brother beat me to church! I was so excited because he did not really go to church much when we were little and growing up at home. I told God that He didn't have to do anything else for me in my life because this was a long time prayer answered. I can happily give God glory now and say that we can talk on the phone, share emails, and love on each other's children and on each other. God can mend all relationships.

Back to the family reunion in 2000. My man was on his way to spend his second weekend in jail. I had a cell phone so on our way back from Louisiana my man had explained he was going to get a ride from jail. My brother, his wife, my niece and I had ridden together to Louisiana. When we got back Harold was about to pull out with the car. He had a very feminine guest with him in the passenger seat. I knew her and I got out and said what is going on honey? He explained she needed a ride somewhere and they were going to pick up some weed. I met him smoking weed so it wasn't his thing to stop just because I had stopped and was pregnant. He knew just about the only thing that would make me leave him is if he smoked in the house. That would make me leave real quickly because nobody was going to pollute my baby. That was embarrassing but I had gotten good at hiding it, so I thought. I was thinking to myself, "How could someone love me, spend time in jail and then get out and immediately spend time with another woman. She looked a hot mess too. But she was thin, and I always thought that being fat was the reason I could not get a good man. When I got off the medicine from being healed from that blood disease I had gotten up to 270 lbs. Now I was big and pregnant and I was convinced I was definitely unattractive.

Later that year in September I began to have problems with my pelvis. It was beginning to spread early and threaten my body to deliver the baby early. I was treating my body so well that I just knew that God would not let that happen. One day I had to get my dad to pick me up from work because we could not get in touch with my man and he took me to the hospital. People thought I was going to deliver the baby. She was not due until December 13th which is my brother's birthday. How about that? My doctor met me at the hospital and told me that I had been infected with a sexually transmitted disease. You read that correctly. I was mortified. My doctor was this little 60-year-old Indian lady and boy was she fierce. She was so pissed off she told me to come to see her that Monday and to make sure I brought my husband with her. Fortunately, it was a disease that was cured with 4 huge pills.

When we got to the doctor's office she went smooth off on my man and I gladly let her. She told him to get tested for everything that she had placed on a list and told him he better bring the results to her because she knows that didn't come from me. She explained to him that she tests me every visit because she is concerned about me and the baby; and, I was fine last visit so she knew the disease was not from my doing. Now I had to report to CPS when the baby was born to make sure no harm was done to the baby. That disease could have caused my baby to born blind. I give God the glory on that one. I told God I know she won't because I have been treating my body well and the baby didn't do anything to deserve this and I pray over her every day and sang her a song I wrote just for her every day. My daughter was born with her eyes wide open and so big. (I am cheesing finally in this book!)

That Thanksgiving I woke up pretty upset because I couldn't go to Louisiana to be with family like always. The good idea was to go to my sister-in-law's family gathering. This was really a good idea. When my man and I got there I walked in and the love exuded all over that house. It was a nice alternative after all. Let me take a break for a minute and be real. I put my hands together and I Prayed and asked God for guidance and strength to go into this next area. Ok so now let's keep going. When I got to the house and settled down I noticed my phone had a message on it so I listened to it. This is how the message went that was on the phone:

"Hey, this is me. I am just going to come clean to my man about everything. I love him and he is trying to work it out with me. I can't take any more of this relationship we have. I hope I didn't give anything to my husband. You need to come clean with your wife too. I hope you didn't give her anything too. So call me whenever but this is over."

I am not kidding. Just like that on the morning of Thanksgiving right when I started to smile a little. My baby was due the next month so I was really big and everyone there was so excited for both me and my sister. I looked across the room at my man and he looked like he knew something was really wrong with me. I got up and told him I needed to talk outside. We went outside and I asked him about the message. See my man and I shared my cell phone. I shared my everything with him. He just looked at me like I was crazy and out of my mind. Don't you know he stood there and didn't say anything but, "I'm going for a walk." Just like that. I watched him walked down the street while lighting a cigarette and when he disappeared into the distance I turned around and force my tears to internalize and I walked back into the house and sat down by God – I hoped.

To my delight, I sat down by a true diva and a seriously awesome woman who was used by God to talk to me. Wisdom can see just about anything even if you try to hide it. She engaged me in a conversation about who I was and had heard that I could sing. Because that is a happy place for me I could talk about that. She asked me what I was doing and I explained really nothing but living at the time. She asked me about school and I realized that I wasn't going to be married for too much longer because my husband obviously was not going to stop sleeping with other women. At that moment I felt really stupid for not taking my studies seriously at the University. I realized even if I had gotten my mind right I have graduated by now or at least be close. But no I was not doing anything. The more I thought about that statement the more I got depressed and mad at myself. She brought me back to the moment by saying, "You know you can get back in school even if you have a child, right?" I said nothing. She continued, "Come see me when you get you head on straight ok?" I looked at her defeated and said, "Ok I sure will." I was sitting next to Bernadine Oliphant of Houston, Texas. She became my mentor at that moment and I didn't even know it. I truly thank God for her fearlessness of addressing someone she didn't even know right in the middle of what she saw on me. That is what I meant when I earlier said that seasoned women need to 'talk' to and share with younger women.

When my man and I got back that night he left and didn't come back until the morning. I didn't fight and I didn't fuss. I accepted that this was crazy and I was caught in it and I didn't think I could get out of it. The great thing about my man is he did keep a job around that time because he was able to hustle on that job. He never apologized for what he did. I am not sure if he was embarrassed and that is why he didn't or that he didn't feel I deserved it. I think perhaps a bit of both. I still believe somewhere there is a really good man in there somewhere that wishes could exist in him.

On December 9th that year I got a horrible feeling in my body and it was mild but definitely there. My brother came to pick me up and take me to the hospital. He actually held my hand on the way. I was examined and then sent home because that was the beginning of labor and I was nowhere ready to deliver. The contractions became much stronger by that Monday so I went to the Doctor's office. She examined me and said that I need to walk because the baby was still too high. My mother had taken me to the doctor and that was very nice. I hope you are noticing that all of these trips someone took me that was not my husband. Moving on, I ended up walking around the block with my mother holding a stick in my hand. I was looking like a female pregnant Moses in a moo-moo dress. (Smile) Can I tell you that I did not care too?

I had been spending the night at my mother's house so I could have someone near me and she and her husband took turns staying up with because you can't sleep through contractions. My man would come at some point in the night and relieve my stepfather at the time. By Monday afternoon my contractions had been about 15 minutes apart. My doctor advised me not to go to the hospital until they were 5 minutes apart. So I had been in labor for 3 days at this point and highly exhausted. Thank God I was crazy enough to eat something when everybody fell asleep. My mother told me not too because I would throw up but I was so thirsty. So I put a can of peaches in the refrigerator. When it was cold enough I started eating them and drinking the juice for dear life! My mother must have felt me because she entered into the kitchen right when it all came up, which, was about 1 minute after I had started eating. She started screaming, "It's time for the baby, it's time for the baby!!"

My man drove me to the hospital at maximum speed and the nurse came out with a regular size wheelchair. I told them I would not be able to fit in that thing and they were crazy enough to tell me to try. So to shut them up I tried. I couldn't fit. Therefore, I blew their heads off with my comments of course. I got up to the room at about 6 am. I was ready for the epidural to numb this now 4-day pain. Because I had the history of ITP I was told they had to do a platelet count on me first. What!! They drew blood around 9 am. The results did not come back until 12 pm. Jesus I was in so much pain and I had not slept since the Friday night before. I finally got the epidural around 3 pm. Lord have mercy. I can just feel some of you saying, 'Oh my God!' (Smile) I remember the anesthesiologist telling me that the whole process would take about 15 minutes but that depended on me being still. I am here to tell you it took that man 7 minutes. He was so tickled that he laughed a little. I told him I had great incentive to be still and that was NO MORE PAIN. When he began to run the medicine into my system he looked at me and said, "How do you feel?" I said to him, "I love you." He smiled and said, "I know." I said, "No, you don't understand, I really really love you. Thank you so much I just love....," and I faded away into one of the deepest sleep I have ever experienced.

I remember a little nurse saying, "It's time to push." I looked up and everyone was there. All the nurses, the doctor, and my husband. So I started pushing. It took me 5 minutes to get that girl out of me. She was born 8 lbs and 7 oz and 21 in. long. It was about 9:30 pm now and my brother was at the door saying, "Just hold on Vawn it's almost 12 so she can be born on my birthday." If I could have I would have gotten up myself to touch him. (Smile) I remember the doctor slamming her down on my belly and I just started crying and proclaiming, "My baby!" The staff cleaned her up and gave her to my man. He stood in front of the bed and I had just enough strength to lift my head a little to see her looking up at him holding her. I starting singing our song and then the most incredible thing happened. My daughter turned her 15-minute old head to me and looked me square in the eyes. Her eyes were opened! They were not damaged from that awful STD! And she sighed when she saw me as if to say, "Aw yes, there she is." I love my baby. She is just like me too.

They took her to the nursery and I said a prayer as they left and my brother, friends, and family kept running to me to tell me how smart she was. They told me how big her eyes were and the doctor told me how healthy and perfect my baby was. Thank you, Jesus. After all, she had witnessed in the womb; she was still fearfully and wonderfully made. I remember them giving me another shot that would cause me to sleep. I was so grateful. I told the orderly to please bring me some food. She told me that I shouldn't eat because I might throw it up. I said, "Girl please bring me something and don't play because I want some real food. I hadn't eaten in 5 days. What is my baby going to suck out of me?" They brought me chicken fried steak, country gravy, mashed potatoes, a roll, broccoli, and my favorite – apple juice that was almost frozen. I knew I was going to hold that food down because I am a country girl and that is my favorite meal. I gobbled it up in 7 minutes because that medicine held me captive. That morning about 5 am a nurse brought me my baby and said, "She misses you."

Not many women in my family were able to breastfeed and I prayed that I would be able to do so. My prayer was answered. My baby took to my breasts just fine. Later the CPS doctor came to examine her and the only reason I didn't curse somebody out is because my baby was watching me and I didn't want to show her something crazy so I let him make it. He told me she was clear of any issues and I boldly told him, "I know that." He left because I am sure I looked like a pissed off black woman and I did not care at all.

We went home 2 days later and began our life together. She wouldn't go to anyone, not even her daddy unless I gave him one of my shirts to put over his chest. She needed my smell. She still does. Even now I can just look at her and she will run to hug me. Oh, I love my baby. I had decided I couldn't be a good mother if I stayed with my man. I didn't want her to end up like me and my mother. You know, with a man that didn't love us the way we should be loved. I figured if I stayed I would teach her to do just that. So I decided in my head that it was time to go. But what about my marriage vows?

Dear Sis,

I know that I am completely blessed to have given birth to such a healthy and forever feisty little angle. My daughter is truly a prophet. There is not much to say here because this entire part of my life speaks for itself. I had begun to know now that this relationship was truly a problem and was scared because I wanted to stay married forever. I know that it was my mother's bravery and tenacity to leave a very harsh relationship that gave me the courage to leave early and break the cycle. No, I am not encouraging divorce and the idea to give up. But we are not talking about a godly marriage. Neither are we talking about two saved people here. We are talking about one trying to get closer to God and one living completely like hell. This was a volatile situation and was going down so fast and at this time I was starting to see clearly. I wouldn't have to suffer and raise my children in the comfortableness of that suffering.

I know that I was blessed because it wasn't HIV that my husband gave me. I began to pray more and I started thinking about God more. I was more depressed than ever but because I had my daughter now, the determination in me began to come alive again. Honestly, I had given up on my husband loving me and treating me better. I just stayed in my fantasy world that somehow it would maybe get better. In my right mind, I knew better. Now we had a beautiful daughter and thought I would be trapped in this volatile relationship forever even though I did want out. I knew there is no way I could go because of God hating divorce.

Isaiah 10:9-10 New King James Version

Remember the former things of old, For I am God, and there is no other; I am God, and there is none like me, declaring the end from the beginning, and from ancient times things that are not yet done, saying, 'My counsel shall stand, and I will do all My pleasure.

Chapter 10 – Starting to See

I was not able to return to work because I had been out so long with complications before my daughter was born, that I ran out of medical leave time. The decision was to let me go. Fortunately, my man was working and he did hold it down for a long time. I had found another job and it seemed to be going well. I had been working at this job for about 2 months and I really liked what I was doing. Not as much as music but I did prefer this work at the time. On my way to work one morning I was stopped by the police for speeding about 8 miles over the speed limit. I was nervous and told the truth that I knew that I was speeding but I was a little late to work and they arrested me anyway and took me to jail. I had a seatbelt ticket that turned into a warrant that I had completely forgotten about. I got that ticket in the fall of 1999 and it was the spring of 2001. I could not believe I had handcuffs on me. I cannot describe the nervous feeling that captured me.

When I arrived at the jail I was given a chance to use the phone. I called my husband and he did answer thank God. We did not have money because we spent everything that came in and there was not a lot coming in any way. We truly lived in a poor man's mentality. I called my mom to tell her what had happened and she said that she would try to keep in touch with my man but that she was sure he could handle it. Now let's take a break right there. My mom could have come to get me out of jail right that second but she didn't. She told me she couldn't do anything to help me at that time. She told me that out of all the many, many times I had used her, my dad, my brother and anyone I could find to get him out of jail surely he would work in my favor now because now it is his turn. My husband did not have any ties to the community like I did as far as having a family. Was he going to call his parents to get me out of jail like I had called mine? Was he going to call his sibling to get me out of jail like I had mine? Was he going to get money from anywhere like I did? My husband had warrants still at this time so he could not come to visit me. I was told that if he didn't come to get me soon I would be transferred to the Harris County Jail. Sure enough, I was transferred to Harris County.

As I arrived at the new jail I thought about how many times I had picked my husband up and how quick I manipulated to get him out. He never spent more than 4 hours in jail if I could help it. I remember once I had my mother out at 2 am in the morning getting him out of jail. We turned the wrong way on a street and thought we were about to die because a car was headed straight for us. It turned out to be a police officer. My mom explained to him that we were trying to get someone out of jail and we were confused about the directions and were unfamiliar with this part of town. The officer explained how to get back on track and we did just fine after that. I also thought about all of the horror stories my man and the TV had told me about jail. Fear had total control over me at this point.

When I got inside they took the handcuffs off of me and I sat and waited. I felt so out of place in there. I was put in a holding cell that was about the size of a child's room. It was about 45 women in there as well. There were an open toilet, a sink and something that looked like a water fountain in there. For your pleasure of seating, there was a wall length cement bench. I had on a black skirt with a split, high-heel multi-colored sandals, a white blouse and a red suit jacket to match. Fortunately, I did not have on any makeup that day. I had always struggled with claustrophobic tendencies so I was truly suffering the moment the doors closed. I had just ended a period 3 days prior and was glad about it. I was sitting there holding on for about 3 hours when anxiety started to kick in. I had to use the bathroom so bad but of course, I was uncomfortable about going in front of everyone that was in there so I held it. Then I felt something leave my body. I had to go sit in the cold and steal toilet. When I looked down I noticed that I was bleeding!

So I took a bunch of toilet paper and rolled it together to make a poor woman's pad. I went to the small crack in between the wall and the sliding door and hollered, "I started my period and I need some pads!" Someone hollered back, "You all will go see the medic eventually so just hold on!" Hold on? I thought to myself like, "I'm bleeding mutha----!" I wasn't saved back then. I told myself I was in jail now and there ain't (yes – ain't) no telling when I am going to get out of here. Therefore, I may as well adjust. I kept my nose pressed in that little open crack to the world as long as I could stand. I was hot and uncomfortable. I was cramping and then the thought came to me, "when is my man coming to get me out?" I felt like I had been there for more than a day.

All of a sudden the door started moving so I had to move and went to sit back down. The nastiest looking woman rolled in with her precious self. Somebody loves her and if that is not a person on this planet, God does. There were plenty of whores and junkies there. I am thinking about that now. I can't believe I had been exposed to that enough to be able to recognize what I saw. There was a doctor there as well and she told me she had forgotten about a ticket as well and waiting for someone to come and get her. There was a jailhouse comedian there trying to get folks to laugh. I was thinking, "None of this stuff is funny to me chick!" I had taken off my jacket and the crack head came to me and asked me if she could use my jacket. I almost bit her head off when I told her, "No! Are you kidding?" She backed away apologizing. Life had beaten me up so bad that was used to biting back to keep from being hurt first. I don't know why I didn't apply that to the relationship I was in. Most women who are in these types of relationships have juice everywhere but where they should.

I was disgusted because the guards had gotten pissed off at the women and stopped checking us in. So we had to wait even longer to get up to our cells and beds. Everyone was waiting to get to the cell to be more comfortable. Please! At that time some of us were released to go to the medic to record what medicines would be needed. I heard people say they had HIV, AIDS, herpes, diabetes and all kinds of stuff. I walked up to the window and said, "Nothing. But I just started my period can I please get some pads?" In the driest and most monotone voice, she replied, "You'll get your supply when you get to the cell. Next!" Just like that.

When I got back to the holding cell I changed my toilet-paper-pad again and sat down feeling nasty and defeated. The door opened and I was one of the names to get called out to go get checked into the system. When I got to the window I was told I had already been checked in at the first jail I was at and I could have already been in the process to getting to a cell. Therefore they put me with a new group to head to the cell. I took the time to enjoy not being in that closed in space for a few minutes. That may have seemed completely messed and fowl because I would not have had to sit in that tight little holding cell for so long. However! It was a blessing. I didn't realize night had come! So I feel blessed that I didn't have to spend a night in jail around women who may want my sweet stuff.

We ended up having to take an elevator down to the bottom floor to get our orange suits. I hated elevators more than that tiny holding cell. When we got into the area to check in our clothing we were told to line up. First, we had to take off all of our clothing in front of one another. Then we were told if we had on white cotton bra and panties we could keep those on and if not we had to take off our underwear. I had on black nylon bra and panties. I was so nervous about telling the guards what was going on and they didn't look like they wanted to talk. So I said nothing. I was so funky they started spraying air spray all around me. I still said nothing. I was standing there being necked with a roll of toilet paper clinging to flesh and truly holding on. Then they handed us the orange pants and shirts. Kindly enough, we were given jail-house slippers. I put everything on. When one of the guards stood by me to tell us to line up to go to another holding spot I whispered to her that I started my period and could she please give me some pads. She did and told me to put them inside of my pants and not take them out until I get to the cell. I did what I was told.

We got to another area and we were told to wait again. I will break for a minute here. I did not know that God was still taking care of me right at that moment. It usually does not take that much time to get to a cell. God was protecting me from having to spend the night in a cell that had no protection. Back to the story. We were all sitting there trying to hold on. We all eventually went to sleep and the lights were turned off but we could still see. After a long while, someone came to take us to our cells. Now I was arrested one morning and by the time I got to the cell it was the next morning. I could tell because some girls were taking showers in the open shower and brushing their teeth. I had been in jail for a full day already. Where was this man at?!

I was given a thin mattress, one towel, and a toothbrush and I watched the doors close behind me. Some women are spending a lifetime in jail and someone year. Check this out – one minute was too long for me. So I pray for the women that spend any more time than that. I pray for everyone that spends more time than one minute. I dropped my things and went to the public toilet and had to do more than tinkle and I handled my business like I wasn't ashamed at that point. God truly made me an adapting fighter. Thank you, God. Girls passed me by like it was nothing and I didn't say anything either. Even though I didn't have underwear, I had a pad now. Yes! So I wrapped the toilet paper around that and it was more durable so I felt a tad more protected.

I was put in what they call an 'animal tank'. This is a large cell that housed maybe 20 women. I suppose that was better than the one with one or two people. I went to find and open cot to put my mattress on. I found one. As I walked to it a big chick passed by me and then said, "You smell gooooood." I thought to myself as I kept walking and didn't respond, "Oh Lord please save me from having to spend the night here."

When I got to my bed I lie down on my mattress and lay on top of it. I put my towel on my arm and put my face in my towel so that I could cry without anyone noticing it. Then I heard the deep Berry White- like voice say, 'Whatchu in fo?" I looked up confused and looking for a man and saw this chick looking at me and waiting for her answer. I decided not to lie because I have always been told I tell the truth with my face and because I am a cute girl I didn't want to add to the fire, "I am in here for warrants." She said, "Oh for real? You will probably get out then pretty quick." I said nothing. I realized that there are women who were NOT getting out. I decided to get strong and deal with the fact that I probably would not get out until my time was served. I cried some more. I got up to go to use the phone and collect call somebody.

As I approached the phone this old black lady who clearly did not have all of her right minds began to befriend me. I talked to her for a minute. Then this white lady came and screamed, "Don't talk to her? She will get you raped (she said something else) and she is crazy as hell!" I took that advice and went to the phone. I was told by one of my husband's women that he was working on getting me out. I am laughing and crying now! Oh, my God, I can't believe I lived like that! (And please don't judge me and say I am some kind of fool. Plenty of women, including maybe the women reading this book, have done some really stupid stuff in a relationship. It is not a good situation if it ain't a God Good situation.) Can you believe she was letting me call her collect to keep in touch with the outside world? She told me I could call her as much as I wanted and I did. She was allowing him to use her car and her brother or friend was helping him. Then we were told to line up to do a count. This count is to make sure no one had escaped. Then the guards started. I noticed they would say the last name of the inmate and the inmate would say a number. I had no idea what that number was. I began to look at my wrist where they had placed a band that looks like the ones you get at a hospital. I saw all kinds of numbers. I picked one and asked the Lord to help me say the right one. See at this time no one could figure out this cute girl. They had no idea if I had been to jail before or not because I was acting like I had. I was not walking around fronting or anything, I was just surviving and adapting. Wouldn't you know that when they yelled, "Stearnes" I called out the correct number? Or the guard smelled rookie on me and let me make it. I am sure that confused some of the women that were trying to figure me out even more. Thank God again.

So now they were bringing lunch. I don't remember what we ate and I don't give a crap either. (Smile) I do remember I had chips and I will tell you why. A little sweet-looking white pregnant girl came up to me and asked me if I was going to eat my chips. As I looked at her like I wanted to bite her head off I said, "Yes!" She said, "Ok my bad girl I was just asking." And she moved on and never came back. I wasn't trying to be mean or front like I was hard or something. I was hungry! I felt bad but didn't apologize because this was jail.

When I finished eating I saw a guard and went to her and explained that I was bleeding and I wasn't supposed to be in jail and my man was getting me out. She told me to let her know when the fees for my charges were paid and she would let someone know. I was whispering to her so it could be between me and the guard and I think she respected that. Hours passed and I was growing more hopeless and nervous. I looked at the TV and watched it for a while to get away. I called the girl again and she said that he had finally paid the bill to get me out. I was thinking, "Ok he does love me." I think he did love me somewhere but not with God's love; which, is the kind of love a husband should have for his wife and a wife for her husband. That is order.

I saw a girl working on the outside collecting lunch plates and called her over to me. I told her that the guard told me to tell her when I heard something and could she please let her know it was paid. I was begging like an R&B singer from the 70's. (Smile) She came back to tell me to get a piece of paper and she would give it to the guard. I thought to myself, "great how I am going to get a piece of paper?"

It was now dinner time and they were handing out dinner plates. I got my plate and then I went to the crazy old black lady and I told her I had something for her. She came and sat by me and brought all of her stuff. She carried all of her stuff with her at one time. I noticed it earlier and she had paper and pens. I told her that she could have anything on my dinner plate if she gave me a piece of paper and a pen. She was happy to accept. I quickly wrote out my information from my bracelet and gave it to the girl working. Thank God it was the same one. She did give it to the guard and I watched her do it. I called my man's other woman and she told me she would let him know. She explained that her friend and brother were driving my man to the jail to pick me up.

I saw the sun setting and started tapping my nails to my teeth. I was truly about to break out running when I heard, "Stearnes get your stuff time to go!" THANK YA!! I grabbed my things so fast and pressed my face against the bars so hard that when they opened I barely had enough time to move so that I would not get my face crushed. I was out of that animal tank. I was taken to what looked like a cafeteria setting. There was this sweet little Mexican girl sitting there crying. She said to me as I approached her to sit down, "Please don't be afraid of me. I won't hurt you."

I sat down by her and told her I was not. I still had an attitude and that made her cry. I realized I was on my way out so I told myself to calm down. She started crying on my shoulder and I asked her what she was in for. She explained to me that she had killed her sister-in-law! I was shocked but not scared. I had gotten used to some things being in the relationship I was in. She told me she was 19 years old and she had been having problems with her sister-in-law. Apparently, the sister-in-law had threatened her little boy and had been abusing him. She went to confront her sister-in-law and just wanted to scare her so that she would stop and she had a knife. Things got out of hand and she stabbed her sister-in-law. The sister-in-law bled to death. She said she felt bad because her children will never again see their mom but my kids will be able to see again. I was speechless. In my head, I was remembering when I had done some similar things that could have landed me in the very same place. When you are afraid and abused that is a really scary place to be in. There is but one way to save you from reacting in those situations and that is the love of God. Only His love will keep your thoughts sober. Thus, I just hugged her.

I wanted to know how much time she was given to serve and she said they had first given her 35 years. Her grandmother had decided to fight the case with the court-appointed attorney and the decision was changed. I thought I heard her say it was changed to 15 years. I said, "That is better because now you will be out when you are 34." She said, "No I said they gave me 50 years!" She, of course, cried harder than ever. Then an inmate that was moping came over and asked what was going on and I explained everything. She hugged her and told her she was going to have to stop crying if she was going to be able to hang in there. Someone arrived to take me to a place to get my clothes back on. I told her I would always pray for her and I promise I still pray for that girl. Always. That could have very well been me sitting there. That could be any of us sitting there who has ever entertained the emotion of fear and hate.

I got my clothes on and my underwear thank you, Jesus! I sat in another holding cell perfectly content because I was getting out. All of the girls were happy because they were getting out too. There was someone singing and tearing up my trained ears with an awful noise I'm telling you. Then she asked if I could sing and I told her yes. So they were all preparing for me to sing something and I kept stalling. Then my name was called for me to leave right when I was going to actually sing. I jumped up without even saying I'm sorry I couldn't sing. Some of them had the nerve to look disappointed. What? Was I supposed to stay and perform? This ain't the jailhouse rock! Ok. Whatever honey, I was out of there.

I had arranged for my man to meet me 4 blocks away because I didn't want to sit in front of the jail. And besides, he had warrants as well so he couldn't be close either. Therefore, I walked 4 blocks to the meeting spot. I sat there as the sun fell down. I looked at the sky dripping with rays of fuchsia, gold, purple and clouds have drawn creatively; and, I thought how beautiful God is to give me the ability to see color. All of a sudden, those colors turned to gray as I realized I had been in jail for almost 2 days and that I had never let my man sit there that long. I was looking forward to seeing my baby which that thought had tormented me the entire time I was in jail. The babysitter had kept her for me. Lord Jesus my daughter had been through some things and been protected even more.

When an unfamiliar car had arrived and pulled up to stop I got so excited because I knew my man would be in there. That is a fantasy that kept me going while I was going through this experience. I will be honest. I am crying again. I imagined he would get out of the car and be so happy to see me and hug and kiss me and hold me tight. He got out of the car looking good and untouched. I went to hug him as he dryly said, "Get in the car Vawn." I looked at him and I said, "Can I at least have a hug please." He said that we had to hurry up and get in the car because he had warrants and didn't want to be around that area too long. What was I expecting? He was being driven by his other woman's brother and he was the car.

No one said anything to me and everyone stared straight ahead as the car began to move. I got in and looked out the window the entire ride home. As silent tears trickled down my plump cheeks, I realized I was free from jail but on my way to my real prison.

We went to get my baby and went home. I took an hour long shower. I played with my baby. My husband left to go out or something. I really didn't care. I put my baby to sleep and sat up. I couldn't sleep. I found his weed stash and smoked a huge blunt by myself outside. I came in and took another shower and lay down to sleep.

****

I went to the doctor the next day because I had been having problems with making love to my husband. Because I had gotten an episiotomy when giving birth to my daughter I had to be sewn together. I thought that somehow something was done wrong. Every time we tried to make love he had problems entering into me. The doctor examined me and told me that there was nothing wrong with me. She explained to me that our bodies will not do what it doesn't want to do. Everybody could see that I was in a bad relationship but me. I left feeling so defeated. I knew that my man would go get him some loving even if I was giving him the same. Now that I was having problems I knew he would cheat even more. I forced myself to lay with him. It hurt so badly but I was trying to be a 'good wife.' You know I have to break right now right?

God tells women that we should honor our husbands. Not become a slave to Satan in our marriage. This man was clearly not carrying himself as a saved man of God. I was in danger of getting a disease from his adultery. If a couple really is having problems they should work together to get through them. I did not have to force myself to have sex with my husband if my mind and body were not ready. Clearly, I was being abused so my body would not react if there was no love.

One night, while I was forcing the love making there, came a problem. I had begun to want to leave this very terrible relationship and I did not want to get pregnant again so we used condoms. We were making love in a doggy-style position and something felt strange so I stopped and turned around. This man had taken the condom off without me knowing it. I felt like I had been treated like a nasty whore by my own husband. I asked him why he would do something like that and get me pregnant when he knows I was not ready. We didn't have money. We didn't have anything. He just looked at me like he was stupid or something. I got up and went to take a bath.

About one month later I was coming home from work and when I stepped out of the car I vomited all over the street. I went in to take a pregnancy test and I was indeed pregnant with my seriously handsome son.

Dear Sis,

I know that this was the beginning of me seeing that this relationship was very bad. I still felt like it was hopeless. Now that I was pregnant I would never be able to leave him. This is really all the Lord is leading me to say. If you cannot see how bad this situation is and cannot see what should be done then I pity you. You are in denial and need to get on your knees right now and ask God to show you the truth. Ask God to help you never to allow yourself to be in such a situation. If you are in the situation, ask God to get you out now. I also know that God showed me extreme favor to not be in the same situation as that young girl who was sentenced to live her life in prison.

Jeremiah 29:11 amplified version

For I know the thoughts and plans that I have for you, says the Lord, thoughts and plans for welfare and peace and not for evil, to give you hope in your final outcome.

Chapter 11 – My Second Born

I was worried about being pregnant again. We didn't have a lot of money and didn't have any kind of discipline with saving or spending. I have always wanted several children but at this time I was thinking about finally leaving a crazy situation and trying to get the courage to walk away. I remember going to work and there was a co-worker of mine telling me of how she was only able to have one baby. She begged me not to feel sad about being pregnant again even if I was in a volatile relationship. That was the conversation that turned my fear to happiness. I would much rather be having a baby than not be able to have a baby.

I began to think that this may help my relationship with their father. I would be having his first son. All men want a son right? This would be good right? My man was still smoking weed, drinking and popping pills. I was as healthy as an ox with a baby and another on the way. A new supervisor had stepped on the floor and I got called into the office. I was hoping the news of me being pregnant didn't spread around the office. Sure enough, the news hit the boss. I was asked to clean out my desk because I could not get to work on time. This information was true. I could not get to work on time to save my life. I had plenty of obstacles in front of me as well daily. Now it was up to my husband to keep the bills going for me. I remember one day he came home in the middle of the day from work.

He drove a shuttle for the airport so he had transportation once he got to work. Our car was broken down again. He was getting a ride from the girl that was available when I was in jail. He promised me there was nothing going on between them but friendship. She did too. I promise you women will lie in your face, drive off, and have sex with your man. Let's move on.

This particular day he came home on break was pretty interesting. He brought me money to get groceries. We had limited furniture to sit on. I had one chair in the living room and I believe there were a kitchen table and a few chairs. My man dropped me and my daughter off at the store that was right down the street and we got groceries and walked back to the apartment. That evening he got home about 11 pm. He had gotten off at 6 pm. When he came home late I was always upset; which is a bit goofy to say I was always upset when he always came home late. Women are so good at pushing themselves into a fantasy world. I was just ministering to a lady I met about this yesterday. I asked her, "What has this man done to make you think that he will give you all these things you want? Like security, love, friendship, and loyalty." She began to name me things like calling her every morning, lending her money, her lending him money and letting her meet his family. That is all fine except one thing. The reason why she called me is because she found out that he slept with another woman! HELLO SOMEBODY! I have to laugh. I told her girl you are just like the rest of us who didn't love ourselves and self-blinded ourselves to live in a fantasy. Shall I explain? I thought you would never ask. I will do that and then tell you the rest of what happen when this man came home on this particular night.

Self-blinded into a fantasy is quite simple actually. What happens is we dream and fantasize about the life we want with the man that we love. We latch on to all of the 'good moments' we have shared with this man. In all relationships, there are some good moments. Even the one I telling you about now had 'good moments'. We spent a weekend at the beach once and that was so fun. I remember once I was so sick and on medication from and awful stomach flu that I woke up to my man cleaning me up in the middle of the night. Yes, you read correctly. I had actually lost my bowels all over myself and he actually cleaned me up. Wow! If you can't anything good about someone that hurt you, you are still walking like a victim and you need to stop that mess. How? Pray and truly forgive.

When we fantasize so much that we forget reality is different from that dream world, then that is the problem. We stay on the 'good moments' and live in them and dream in them. Then we continue dreaming up new moments we 'wish' would happen or we are waiting for them to happen. All the while reality is so very different and so very real. This is self-blinded into a fantasy world. So for my girlfriend who I was ministering to, I plainly told her just what I wrote. I also told her that if I man cannot offer you the basic things you are willing to offer him then how is that love. I am not saying he should be just like you. I am talking about trust and commitment. Most men who are not ready for something this mature and real have told you in so many ways they do not want what you want, we just didn't want to listen. Like a child with a finger in each ear singing, la la la, we do not want to hear. That is so detrimental.

Back to the night that my man came home late. Let me tell you this. He carried a cell phone so that I could contact him if I needed to. This was one of the rare moments we had a home phone. I would call his cell phone and if he would answer that would be great. When he would get home he would separate his cell phone battery from the phone and hide it from me so that I could not look at the call history or listen to his messages. He was so stoned this night that he forgot. I was downstairs cleaning up because I could not sleep. My daughter was asleep in her room and my man was passed out in the bedroom. We had a nice stereo at the time so I was jamming when I noticed his cell phone on the table going off. It was about 1 am at this time. I told myself I would not be nosey and answer his phone and let it go to voice mail. After about 30 minutes passed I felt like I was sleepy enough to fall asleep as soon as my face hit the pillow. My man snored heavily and I could not sleep through that noise when I was pregnant so I had to wait until I was literally too tired to stay up to go to bed.

I passed by his phone and picked it up. With my belly big with his son, I stood there in the darkness contemplating on whether or not I should listen. I did. I heard in the sweetest voice, "Hey it's me. I just couldn't sleep without hearing your voice. But it looks like I missed you so just call me whenever. Take care." It's me? Now you know that is deep when you say 'it is me." No introduction needed which means they are truly connected. For the first time, I didn't call her back. Why? I wasn't surprised anymore. I was just hurt and disappointed again. I didn't wake him up. I just sat down and cried. Not hard. I just let the tears run down my face. So much for having a son and that fixing the relationship. At that very moment I felt like I was trapped.

****

We ended up moving in with my brother and his family. I thought this really isn't the life I thought would be leading right now. What happened to me? I am truly barefoot and pregnant. I am uneducated, I have no money, my man don't love me, my brother cheating on his wife, my dad cheated on his and all I do is sit here. Well I got up and got my pregnant self a job. I talked my way into one. The first thing I did was get a car. While I was working I was paying my brother for us to live there. I had complications and stayed in the hospital for four days. I called my boss on her cell phone to let her know. She said she never got the messages. I was fired.

While I was in the hospital for complications, I sat there missing my daughter. It was about the end of September and my man had lost most of his hours at work because everyone was so afraid to fly because of 9-11-01. His check would be about $100.00. Therefore my brother was not getting any money. He was as nice as he could be to me because I was pregnant. I would keep his daughter, my niece. I loved that. Me and the girls. She is like my little baby too. His wife has an older daughter that I am crazy about too. During the day though it was just me and the girls. I taught them ABC's and numbers. We took a nap. We went for walks. Then I prepared dinner for everyone and cleaned. I tried to be a good housekeeper since I was not contributing any money. It's hard to know people are watching you get treated like crap. So when it was time for me to be discharged from the hospital I tried to reach my man. I couldn't find him. I had to swallow and call my sister in law to come and get me. I was so very embarrassed. I just really love her. I love her still.

When I finally got in touch with my man, she was already on the way. He told me he was in a domino game and he had been drinking so it was good that someone else was on the way. I said to him, "How can you do me like this and I have your son in me man?" He responded in his drunken stupor and I did myself a favor and just hung up. My sister got there and she kept it real. For the first time, I could easily see how hurt she was and pissed off with my man for doing me that way. She spoke her peace and I let her. I was never the kind of woman to make excuses for my man out loud. My mom told me "If you have to make excuses for a man, He ain't the one!" I will say it like this, "She ain't never lying!" Smile.

****

I had my son in January. He came four days late but thank God I wasn't in labor for four days this time. I stayed in labor with him only 24 hours. He was 10lbs and 23 in. long! I don't think I ever used newborn diapers on him. He was so pretty I knew I had to get a bunch of blue stuff. Smile. Both of my children are absolutely beautiful. Nothing had changed with my relationship with my man. My sister in law had cleaned up the place for our return and I went to my mom's. I had no idea that she would do that and I really hurt her feelings. I may have apologized to her for that in the past but I just took a break to send her a note so that if I didn't, I know that I did now.

 The babies and I did come back from my mom's much sooner than when I had my daughter. So we returned to my brother's place. One day my man actually went to a routine doctor appointment with me. That doctor is the bomb! If the mother was sick, she would get a prescription too. His thought is, there is no way a baby can be well if the mother is not well. He could see straight through my awful situation too. I started seeing how many people could see me in my mess. It was so embarrassing. What I didn't know is I was that much closer to my healing and freedom. This particular day the doctor complimented me on how healthy both of my children were. I believe this man was Jewish and his wife was from Egyptian I think. Go figure. I mentioned that for a real reason. The doctor excused himself from the room for a brief moment. While he was gone my man looked at me and said, "Are you ready?" He said, "Have you been cheating on me?" I know I must have screamed, "What!? You are asking me if I have cheated on you."

 See before I would just be hurt at his wonderful way of breaking me down and keeping me down. But now I was hurt and pissed. It's a good thing when you can get pissed sometimes. That usually says "I don't deserve that." My man went on to explain to me that our son couldn't be his because his hair was curly and his skin was smooth. He said that he looked like he was Mexican. I am sure that one of those dingle birds he worked with told him something that stupid and one of them was probably one of the women he had been sleeping with. She was probably hoping to get him for herself – just as lost and dumb as I was, poor thing. I cried right there in the doctor's' office. I didn't want to because I knew the doctor would be coming back soon. I just could not stop the tears from flowing. I could not believe that he accused me of cheating after all the many times I knew he cheated on me and the times I didn't know. Lord have mercy. I just said, "Look, man, you know this is your son, I am way too stupid to cheat on you." He just stood there looking at me like I was crazy or something. Maybe I was.

 The doctor came back in while I was crying. He told me a story of a little black baby who was in his care. He said she was born prematurely. He said that in his opinion, which meant a lot to me, that black women are the strongest women on the planet. With all that has happened to black women over time, they remain strong and fight to survive and mostly they do and win at it. I have to be honest. I am smiling from cheek to cheek right now because I did survive and I won! Yes! At that moment, however, I just listened and I did receive it. I didn't know how I was going to fight and win this situation. My man just stood there looking confused. Lord Jesus. He gave my son a clean bill of health and we left.

Soon after I got myself a new job and we decided to get out of my brother's hair. Basically, my brother was sick of freeloaders and I don't blame him one single tiny bit.

Dear Sis,

I am listening to "Never Would Have Made It" by Marvin Sapp. You know I am crunk right? Smile real big for me! I know some of you may not be, but you deserve to be smiling real big too. I know now that because I was actually not cowering down to the ugly he was putting me through anymore meant that it was time for me to start seeing and accepting reality. See that is the big thing. A lot of times we don't accept the reality shown to us.

I know that God was with me all the time and the Holy Spirit was there encouraging me because I began to be ready to receive truth. I still had a road to travel. But I was getting my confidence. Confidence. For the Lord is my confidence.

Joshua 1:5-9 Amplified Version

5No man shall be able to stand before you all the days of your life. As I was with Moses, so I will be with you; I will not fail you or forsake you.6Be strong (confident) and of good courage, for you shall cause this people to inherit the land which I swore to their fathers to give them.7Only you be strong and very courageous, that you may do according to all the law which Moses My servant commanded you. Turn not from it to the right hand or to the left, that you may prosper wherever you go.8 This Book of the Law shall not depart out of your mouth, but you shall meditate on it day and night, that you may observe and do according to all that is written in it. For then you shall make your way prosperous, and then you shall deal wisely and have good success. 9 Have not I commanded you? Be strong, vigorous, and very courageous. Be not afraid, neither be dismayed, for the Lord your God is with you wherever you go.

Chapter 12 – The Big Change

I am so thankful to the Lord for getting me through that last chapter. Soon after we moved my man lost his job and I was holding it down. He introduced me to this guy that he used to work with who sold weed and he lived right down the street so that was convenient. I would love to say that I never smoked around my kids but I did. We did. One day we were at a crack head's house my man knew. Now being naïve I didn't know the man was a crack head. He didn't do that when I was there. One day I was passing the joint and I almost passed it to my daughter. She was standing there with her one-year-old little fingers with the thumb and the forefinger position ready to receive the joint. That freaked me out so bad it blew my high, I grabbed my babies, I left my man, the dog, and ran out of there. That was the last time I ever smoked in front of them. Thank God it wasn't that many but one time is WAY too many times. No excuses, that crap was fowl. You should never do that in front of your children.

I was introduced to this girl whom I would love to give her real name but I can't. Out of all the names, I can't remember I promise I will never forget her name. This woman wasn't saved she was just real. I call her my blessed donkey. That may sound harsh but I promise it is one of the most positive compliments I can give. I love this woman to this day. If she needed anything I would give it to her if I could and if God allowed me. Let me explain 'blessed donkey' before I continue. (Read Numbers 5:5-41 and 2 Peter 2:16) God sent a donkey to this awesome prophet so that he would not continue to walk in ignorance and continue in his insanity. I promise God knows exactly how to meet you where you are if you will just hear Him. God loves us so much that He will use a donkey to get us to hear Him. This is why I call her my bless donkey. She was truly used by God. She wasn't saved but she knew she wanted to be so she was not necessarily walking in godly counsel. However, what God allowed her to walk in got my complete attention.

If I didn't know better I would have sworn that girl was trying to get with me herself but she didn't come at me hard enough for me to think so for real. To move the story along I will let you know when I 'started to hear' her. One night she was coming to drop some weed off to me and the kids were upstairs in the townhome asleep. It must have been about 11:30 pm. My man was supposed to be home about 7 pm. I really had stopped caring whether or not he came home at a decent time. I guess I had gotten used to it. I decided to call him in front of her because I was legitimately concerned about him. You know when you talk on a cell phone the conversation can be heard by someone standing close enough right? This was before the age of the Bluetooth. All I said to the man was, "are you ok." That is it. He blew my head off.

He said to me, "Why in the F are you always bothering me about where I am and when I coming the F home. You get on my GD nerves with that S. That's why I don't like being around your MuthaF A." And then he hung up on me. My girlfriend took a puff of the blunt as we sat on my porch and looked at me with one eye closed because the smoke had gotten in it. She passed me the blunt and I took a long hard puff. I then held it in long enough to feel my lungs burning. I looked up at the sky searching for God and wondering if he still was there and if I could find him for help. I could see every star in the sky and a huge moon. It was beautiful. Then I passed the blunt but she stopped me and said, "Smoke because I have something to tell you."

My stomach began to turn in knots because she had such a strong personality. Now for the sake of proving a point, and only proving a point I am going to be clear about what she said just like I was clear with what my man had told me on the phone. She said, "Vawn if the MuthaF talks to you like that and all you are doing is being concerned about that Punk MuthaF then he is doing something he is not supposed to be F-ing doing! That B is a sorry Son of a B for treating you like that and you have his two D kids! F that sorry Bastard! He ain't S! I just had to tell you because we have been hanging for the past few months and smoking together and I think I can be real with you. I'm not trying to hurt your feelings but I am tired of seeing that N---- do you like that. Don't you know you deserve better? F that punk girl somebody will take care of you and them kids. Don't trip. Now, give me my blunt back. Pass!" That last part may have been funny but the rest was not!

I sat there and let her smoke that whole blunt because my mind was melting at remembering all the things I went through that I didn't have time to mention in this book. It would have been a 400-page novel if I did. Perhaps at seminars, if God allows we will get into the other things. Right now "Slowly" by Jill Scott is playing. How perfectly timed! Love it! Anyway, I decided I was going to finally leave him if God would give me a sign. LOL! Like He had not already. Now that is funny. If you are in a situation like this, one day you will laugh again if you let Jesus in. I promise.

    Abuse is abuse and rape is rape. Abuse truly comes in many forms. I remember the day before I saw AND received the sunlight. I'm still a woman and you know what I mean. Who doesn't want to be held and loved, made love too and comforted? He behaved half way decent for a few days and I remember wanted to make love to me. We began some foreplay. Isn't it strange at that moment I felt like maybe somethings good could turn around? We always hold on to hope even though truth is screaming in our face. And sisters there is nothing wrong with that. You are not stupid. There is nothing wrong with believing for a better change. But we have to listen to our nucleus. That's were God's voice lives inside of us and speaks to us very gently. I remember saying, "Get a condom." There is no way I trusted his cheating behind and certainly did not want to get pregnant again. We were downstairs and I remember him looking down into my eye gently and for a moment I thought I saw the kind eyes I first saw that night in college where we met. He told me to hang on and went upstairs to get one. A married man with a stash of condoms. Lord. At that moment my nucleus rang out to me, "Something is wrong. Check the condom." I can seriously tell you the Lord whispered that to me or His angel. I'm not kidding. *"And he said, Go forth, and stand upon the mount before the Lord. And, behold, the Lord passed by, and a great and strong wind rent the mountains, and brake in pieces the rocks before the Lord; but the Lord was not in the wind: and after the wind an earthquake: And after the earthquake a fire; BUT the Lord was not in the fire and after the fire* **a still small voice**. *(1 Kings 19:11-12)*

    When he came back downstairs with that condom on, I snatched it off of him and took it to the kitchen. Remember in the country when you used to put water balloons on the faucet and fill it up? That's what I did. And like a cartoon that thing swelled up and sprouted out water everywhere! You read correctly. My own husband sabotaged the condom. My heart aches remembering this. I have no idea why I even want to be married and in love even now. I guess it's a desire God gave me. There are days I wish he would just take it away. Nevertheless, I move on. I screamed at him, "WHY WOULD YOU DO THIS TO ME!!? And treat me like some kind of dirty whore? I AM YOUR WIFE!" His response was, "what made you check the condom?" Wow!

My pastor always told us not to receive rejection. I did not know what that meant at that time in my life. I received that day that I was dirty maybe. I don't know. Let's just say I didn't think much of myself. But I thought a lot of my children. As a result I just looked at him, said nothing and walked away.

That next day I heard from my very good friend's husband. We were friends then and we are friends now. He used to encourage me to hang in there with my man because he had a good heart. He just struggled to be a good man so one day he could turn it around. He knew I really loved him though. Anyway, he asked me how I was doing and I told him that things were growing worse and worse. He asked had I been reading my bible. I told him not much at all. He asked if I had remembered what I learned and I told him I did. He said whatever you decide I have your back. I told him I would call him and my girlfriend soon. I meant what I said too. When my man came in from his morning walk he handed me an eviction notice. I forgot to mention that I had lost my job. So because I had been the one working for the past 4 months and supporting all of us, and being cheated on, and being abused mentally and verbally and still being broke as a joke; I was the only one out there looking for a job. I figured it wasn't fair that I am the woman out there busting my behind with a man that didn't appreciate me.

When that paper landed on the table I was amazed at how pissed I was. I thought to myself, "Wait a minute, I'm the woman right? He is the man right? Why has this man handed me the noticed? He needs to get out there and do something!" I didn't say a word though. I looked up and the sunlight was shining so strong in my face like never before. I smiled and told God thank you for the sign. I looked at him and said, "I have had enough. I think it's best for me to go my way and you to go yours. I will never keep you from the kids either as long as you don't act crazy." God must have gone before me and gave him peace because all he said was, "Wow." I'm laughing now. Not baby please don't go, but wow. He did eventually start talking to be about not going but I reminded him of everything and he agreed that we break up.

Here is a great note to the wise. Never procrastinate because it will only cause inconvenience and at worse, it will harm you. One day I had felt horny. Very horny. It had been maybe 4 months since the last horrible moment so I figured I would take a chance. Maybe he would show me he loved me and cause me to stay if I made love to him one more time. Whatever. Listen. The kids were upstairs asleep when we got together. I lay down and he ran upstairs to get a condom. We did go for it and I wanted more because he had a smile on his face. He went upstairs to get another condom. While I lay there to wait something came over me and told me to check the condom. I know now that was God talking to me. So he came down with the condom on and lay over me to start. I said wait just one moment and I snatched that condom off and went to the kitchen. Have you even taken a balloon and tried to make a water balloon using the faucet? Ok well, I did that with the condom. It looked like he had taken forks and poked it all over because the water was sprouting out like a sprinkler. He was in the kitchen by then and I said, "What the freak are you trying to do to me?! Haven't you done enough?!" I blamed myself for that because I knew better. I receive forgiveness for myself for that right now, just in case I haven't given it to God.

He left around 5 pm. I went upstairs and started packing my stuff. I looked into his bag just on a whim because I never went through his things. I found mine and the kid's social security cards! That was another blessing of direction from the Lord. Later that night about midnight he came back very drunk. I asked him why he even bothered to come home and he cursed me out. I couldn't just let him make it and I argued back. Never argue with someone drunk. It escalated to me telling him I hate myself for ever loving him and I wished I never met him if it wasn't for the kids. He got nose to nose in front of my face and hollered at me and I pushed him out of my face and he picked me up and threw me across the room. I weighed about 285 lbs at that time. Then I was about to jump up and fight because I promised myself no man would ever fight me and get away with it. How stupid is that? He had been fighting my heart for years. This man climbed on top of me and held me down with one hand over my mouth to where I couldn't breathe. I felt so powerless after a while I started crying and gave up the fight. If you ever said, "I don't know why she let that man beat on her." That's why.

Powerlessness. He got up off me and started telling me I wasn't gonna leave him with the kids. "You ain't gonna take my kids from me B!" He ran up there and put my son in his carrier and took him outside. We didn't have a car at the time that was running so he was on foot. I had barely any clothes on. I grabbed my keys and locked my daughter in the house and ran after him in the middle of the night. Let me tell you of 3 blessings – cell phone that was on at the time, Father lived 5 minutes away, brother lived 5 minutes away. I called my Dad while running and told him to come quickly. Really I don't know what I said but whatever it was he heard me. I caught up with my man and my son and threw my arms in the carrier and we fell on the ground. He was going to have to kill me to get my baby out of my reach. He couldn't drag me because thank God the liquor was moving out of his system so he wasn't as strong anymore. I screamed, "I called my Daddy and he called my brother and they are on the way." My man left us on the street and kept walking. I picked up my baby and ran back to the house.

Before I could barricade the door he was back and came in. At that time my Dad was there and he brought the police. Lord Jesus. Now we are a TV show. My big beautiful dog stood in front of my man and the police said, "Sir get your dog now or we will." I screamed, "Please don't let them kill Zeus man!" So he told the dog to come to me and he did. The police took him into custody. And my brother walked in. My children, my brother, my dad and the police saw me sitting on my knees on the floor looking so pathetic. I was so terribly embarrassed. Oh, God. I was so embarrassed. My brother showed me the first genuine signs of concern ever and said, "Are you ok?" I couldn't even look him in the face. I said yes and stood up to be strong. My Dad said, "Don't let that MF back in here tonight." I told the police don't press charges just keep him from coming back.

The next morning I called Steve and Lanora. They were there in about 2 hours with a truck and 200 dollars. I left. Enough was enough.

Dear Sis,

I couldn't take the dog with me although I loved him so much. I was moving to my mother's house and she does not do the animal thing. Recently I saw my dog. Seriously after all those years I saw him. That was in 2002 in the late summer and it is now 2010. I cried so hard. It was like seeing a lost child. I couldn't take him though. I shouldn't anyway because it is the past. God taught me that I had not cried about losing him. I finally got my part of this book. I went through so many of these situations without crying or I would blame myself. While I have forgiven all and asked for divine forgiveness for those I hurt, I never cried. So let me dry my eyes real quick.

I know that God blessed me with my girlfriend otherwise I would not have seen the light. Read that scripture about the donkey. It will mention that the prophet's eyes were opened by God. Thank you Jesus! I know that it was purposed for me to leave because God made people available to help me and gave me money because I had zero dollars to my name. Thank God for true friends. I love them so much still. I thank God that He does not give up on His love for us. Even to the point to save us from ourselves even after we reject Him.

Ephesians 1:15-23 New King James Version

Therefore I also, after I heard of your faith in the Lord Jesus and your love for all the saints, do not cease to give thanks for you, making mention of you in my prayers: that the God of our Lord Jesus Christ, the Father of glory, may give to you the spirit of wisdom and revelation in the knowledge of Him, the eyes of your understanding being enlightened; that you may know what is the hope of His calling, what are the riches of the glory of His inheritance in the saints, and what is the exceeding greatness of His power toward us who believe, according to the working of His mighty power which He worked in Christ when He raised Him from the dead and seated Him at His right hand in the heavenly places, far above all principality and power and might and dominion, and every name that is named, not only in this age but also in that which is to come. And He put all things under His feet, and gave Him to be head over all things to the church, which is His body, the fullness of Him who fills all in all.

Chapter 13 – Having the Courage to Climb Back Up

I guess I don't have to tell you how nice it was for me to get through that part. There was a part of me that still wanted to get back with my soon to be former husband for the children's sake. I was open to the idea with counseling and seeing some change in him. I never saw that change and therefore I never got back with him. My former husband did not prove to be a Father to the children or a provider. I was forced to file child support on him. I was not going to because I really didn't think he would provide for them anyway. I promise I am not trying to be ugly when I say that either. It is the truth anyway. Let's move on.

I remember when I had to go to the welfare office for the first time. I did not have a car so I had to get a ride. I was truly without anything. It was just about the most miserable existence I can remember other than what I had just come out of. I sat there in that office with my 1 ½ year old and my 8 month old all day waiting to see someone for emergency food stamps. I have no idea how people get comfortable with that type of living. I just cannot fathom it and I can truly say I have been there and done that so I know what I am talking about. I remember sitting down at the desk and being asked a million questions and having to provide tons of information. I was about to break down crying so I finally had to confess. I told the lady that I felt like such a failure and that I had made such a horrible mess of my life. She said to me, "Sweetheart we have all done that at one point of our lives. But this is what we are here for. People just like you who recognize they are in trouble and that they are ready to help themselves. So we are here to help you get on your feet. This is what these services were intended for. Mother's just like who need a little help. So you should be proud of yourself that you are doing the right thing for your children and yourself." Wow. For a brief moment I really believed her. I received food stamp benefits and $220.00 per month spending money. My children were both in diapers so that was half gone. I had to save money for gas money too. It and went into the hallway where there were no windows and called my dad. I told him that my former was outside and I told him I wouldn't be there. My dad asked how he got there. I told him that he was talking about taking the bus to see me. This would require him to ride about 45 minutes and then walk about 30 minutes to my mom's house. And he did just that.

Our conversation was broken with, 'I hear you in there, Vawn!!! I know you are in the house because I can see you!!!" Now if he could see me he was superman because I was in a spot in the house with no windows and I was whispering so low I could hear squirrels arranging their acorns in trees out back! That was funny. But I am so serious. Maybe it was a demon fueling that for him. My dad said, "Get the hell off of the phone with me and call the police girl!" So I did and the operator stayed on the phone with me for the 2 little minutes it took them to get there. The police asked me what I wanted to do to him. I asked them to make sure he doesn't come back but not to take him to jail. I have NO IDEA why I didn't tell them to take him to jail because I felt highly threaten. I was shaking and crying. But I was scared that when he got out he would really come for me. So here is a note to everyone that has ever judged a woman for not leaving an abusive man. Don't! Fear is a big mother of all grips on a person. It is awful to love a man and be afraid of him at the same time. This is very confusing. At that moment I told God that I didn't want to live like that so please take that fear from me and He did. I told my former when he called that night, that if he ever did that again he would have to deal with God first and God has promised to protect me; and, I will NOT hesitate to put his you-know-what under the jail. My former never pulled that stunt again.

To make that part of the story short I will say that he eventually spent time away in prison unfortunately and when he came out I was hoping that change had taken effect. Not. When he walked in my apartment I saw the word 'No' on him. Seriously. I had been walking with the Lord for two years and was seriously prayed up. I told God what I saw would determine my next move. He was the same. I was officially divorced in 2004 in January. I wasn't happy that my marriage had not worked out but it's not like it was designed by God anyway.

Anyway it was Christmas Eve and I was so depressed about my life. I had not found a job yet and I was grown and living with my mama with my kids. I went outside and took four puffs off of that blunt. I started crying because I figured I needed to check myself into a rehab or something. Then I got terrified at the thought of CPS taking my children from me and I would never get them back.

I ran inside and flushed the blunt down the toilet. I took a shower and cleaned myself hoping to lessen the high. I looked in the mirror completely disgusted at the reflection and went to turn on the TV. I looked for the Christian channels. TD Jakes was on TV talking about a turnaround for the new year and looking forward to the new year and leaving the past behind. I got on my knees and said this praying, "Lord I really am scared right now. I don't know much but I know I don't want to live like this. Please don't let anyone take my children from me. You saved me from that man, please save me from this addiction. If you just can take this from me I promise I won't go back to it. I will live for you. Help me Jesus. Please! Help me Lord! Please help me!" When I looked up and stopped crying, I heard, "It's done." It was done. God is so very faithful. This is the day that I was saved. No church bells or choir singing, no preacher preaching or folks saying, "Amen!", but truly the salvation of the Lord was shown. December 25, 2003 around 11pm I was saved by the spirit of the Lord himself. Glory to God.

Dear Sis,

I know that God was just waiting for me to cry out. It is hard to love a man and need to send him to jail because you are in fear for your life. Well then Vawn, what do I do? Send him to jail. I cannot put that any clearer. I know I didn't but I should have. I cannot and you cannot gage what is in the mind of a person. Especially if you have children know that they need you more that your feelings for a man who has obviously threatened you. Then get a protection order on him. That way if you have to defend yourself you can without harm coming to you from officials. This advice is thin in comparison to the depth of difficulty associated with this type of situation. I know that. However, after all of the red tape, this advice is the bottom line. Mostly, please **pray for guidance and don't be afraid to tell someone to help you.**

Unfortunately family may not believe you so go to a minister of any church and tell them. Plead out and make someone hear you. Above all, DON'T GO BACK! Do not go back to this situation until it changes with time and intense and completed counseling. Please stay prayerful through it all. I always minister to women that when you get sick and tired of being sick and tired, God will be waiting on you. That is so very true. I was truly sick of being high. See God had been changing me and I was trying to stay in the old man's ways. But that didn't fit anymore. Where being high comforted me in the past, only God's presence and His word was becoming comforting.

Isaiah 51:12-16 New King James Version

I, even I, am He who comforts you. Who are you that you should be afraid of a man who will die, and the son of a man who will be made like grass? And you forget the Lord your Maker, Who stretched out the heavens and laid the foundations of the earth; you have feared continually every day because of the fury of the oppressor, when he has prepared to destroy. And where is the fury of the oppressor? The captive exile hastens, that he may be loosed, that he should not die in the pit, and that his bread should not fail. But I am the Lord your God, Who divided the sea whose waves roared — The Lord of hosts is His name. And I have put My words in your mouth; I have covered you with the shadow of My hand, that I may plant the heavens, lay the foundations of the earth, and say to Zion, 'You are My people.'

Chapter 14 – Effects that Could Last

This will be a true turning point. Remember what I said about every cause has an effect and every choice has a consequence? I promise you I don't want to tell this part. But I am because I just really want my sisters to know that you are not alone; and, hopefully not to make some of the same choices I made. Mostly, I would love for us to think about our actions before we commit them. That November for Thanksgiving I went to Baton Rouge with family. I guess my cousin picked up on the fact that I needed to get out so she offered to have me go out and just hang like girlfriends with her. We ended up at a club Lord Jesus. There was some music playing and I totally didn't have any confidence in myself for so many reasons. I was now a single mother with no money and no education. I was fat! I was living with my mom and for the first time in my life, I had no dreams and no goals at all. So the DJ played a song that I thought was jamming and I went to the dance floor and started grooving by myself. Before I knew it some guy was dancing with me. I thought to myself, "Oh wow somebody thinks I'm hot enough to dance with."

Because he wasn't trying to grind me I guess I considered him pretty cool. When it was time to close we went out into the parking lot to head for the car. The guy that I danced with was trying to get my attention and so I turned around to talk. At the moment I really can't remember the detailed conversation. I remember him mentioning that my eyes were so beautiful in the moonlight. I really liked that compliment but let's take a break for a minute. I teach my son and daughter to complement each other heavily. One of the reasons I do this is because I figure that if they are used to hearing compliments from the opposite sex when they are actually approached by someone that is interested in courting them, they will be used to the regular worldly way of gaining attention. To be clear let me explain my point. If a boy was to tell my daughter, "Oh you are so beautiful and your skin is so soft," she would say, "And?" My husband, son and I tell her that enough. He will not be able to woo her with the 'okkydoke.' (Which means normal compliments that would only truly grab the attention of someone who never hears it. This is how I was back then.)

See had I been used to hearing that I was beautiful from my father or brother perhaps a man would have to work a little harder to get my attention. That is not to cut them but just to keep it real. When God's love comes into your life and you allow yourself to receive it, then He is your compliment. Let's move on. So Nicolas got my quick attention. He asked me to call him but I told him that I lived in Houston so there was no need to keep in touch. He told me he didn't care because he would travel to see me because I was special. Girl, please! How does he know I am special? Anyway, the man gave me all his numbers. When I got back to Texas I did call him. We talked for a while and I discovered that he had his Bachelor Degree in Biblical Studies and a Masters in Theological History. I may be off on the titles of the degrees but to be plain, the man knew about the Lord. Because of this fact, I told myself that he was 'special.' Catch that because I don't want you to miss it.

I considered him 'all that' because he was a 'man of God.' He called me when he said he would call me and that truly impressed me. I thought I was special to him for real. One day he decided to come and visit me. I really thought I had it going on because he drove from Louisiana to Texas to spend time with me. It was a very cold January day. The sun was out so I didn't mind the cold air one bit. I had decided early that my children would not see any man I dated because they had already lost their father I didn't want them to get confused. Nicolas came to visit me while they were at daycare. We went for a walk in the park and that was great. I enjoyed his conversations because we talked about God and I shared some of my issues with him. All I was doing was giving him fuel better know how to misuse my vulnerable love. That night when the kids went to sleep I rode with him to find his hotel stay. I ended up staying a while and we slept together. Just to make sure no one misses this, we had sex. Again, I thought I was special because he held me for a little while. I went back home feeling 'special.'

It took him four days to call me back after his visit. I had written him a letter that morning and put it in the mail. I explained to him how awful it was for him to use me that way. It would have been nice for him to treat me like a lady because he was a man of God I expected more. I was so hurt and disappointed that he wasn't ready to love me. Let us take a break shall we? That is so lost and naïve. This man did nothing to me. He came and had sex with me because I let him. I could have given him directions to the hotel because it was right up the street anyway. But no, I had to go because I wanted to give him what I thought he needed because that is what I had grown to learn from the world. How could I expect this man to treat me like a queen when I wasn't treating myself like one? To be completely real there is no way a man that would come to town to screw a woman would be accountable to call her. I was too ignorant to know that he just wanted a fling from me. I suppose the love making felt good because when he called me he used a good amount of game on me to keep me hooked.

    He said some mess to me like I should be ready to give us time to get to know one another. He said that he was impressed with me because I showed him at the club that I didn't need a man and that I could be a woman all by myself and he was attracted to that. I really didn't know how I showed him that, but ok. I ate that mess right up. I felt like he knew me. Therefore we continued to talk and he did come through town again about two months later and the same thing happened. He would call me and say, "Do you want some company because I am going to be in town? You know I have been missing you and I can't wait to see you." He would tell me how good the love making is.

    Well, here it goes. During Resurrection Sunday weekend (most commonly referred to as 'Easter') my family and I get together for a small family reunion. The Bible says nothing about Easter, therefore I call it what it is – Resurrection. I will not allow the world to cheapen the reason why I have life which is Jesus dying on the cross and then being resurrected from the dead. Hello, somebody? Let's move on. This particular weekend my mother and her husband got us all a hotel room. Us being myself and children. I called Nicolas and told him where I would be staying which was about an hour away from where he lived. And he came in a hurry. He waited of course until my parents were gone out to have fun for themselves. I told him I didn't want my children to ever see him until he got truly serious about me because I didn't want them to get confused. He was good with that because that meant he always had to come around creeping hours. I didn't see that truth then.

    He did come to the hotel and I let him in. I had just started working for much less than I had made in years and I had to take the job. I still didn't have much money. Oh God give me strength. My children were sleeping hard because they had a really good day playing with their family. I allowed myself to be given to this man in the hotel room with my children right there sleeping. I considered it 'so good' too. He left soon after and left his wallet. I called his family to tell them he left it and he came back. I looked in there and it was 2 fresh 100 dollar bills. I thought about it for a second. You know, not to call, but I was too goofy not to. I should have let him figure it out. But I 'loved' him now. I told y'all I was an underpaid whore.

On the way back to Texas the next day I found myself cramping. I was afraid this man had gotten me pregnant. The next morning I had to go and get me some yeast infection cream. Then I had started to get a cold. By Thursday which was four days later, what I thought was a yeast infection was not. Friday morning I woke up with blisters on my vagina. I called the doctor and had to suffer through the weekend for the appointment I made on Monday. After a pap smear the doctor came in and said to me, "You have genital herpes." I felt like somebody put me in front of a Mac Truck and force me to look while it ran right into me. Oh God I felt so dirty. The doctor said to me as I cried hard, "Vawn, this will not determine the success of your life. Properly treated you will not die from this. This will not determine when you graduate, this will not determine what kind of car you drive, and this will not determine how many bridesmaids you have in your wedding. You will be ok. I will prescribe you something that will help."

I left the doctor's office not believing anything she had just said but with a small prayer of hope. Ultimately the next time he came to visit I told him to his face while he was trying to pull my pants down. I didn't leave him alone for good though. I wasn't quite smart just yet. He told me he would get tested and he would let me know if it was him. Now my former husband had given me 2 STD's. The doctor told me it can lie dormant inside of you and because I had not been with anyone since my former husband it very well could have been my former, but most likely it was Nicolas. Nicolas came back with the information a few weeks later that said he was 'ok'; which, is bull because we continued to be intimate when he came to town. We did not use protection and he didn't break up with me. So there you have it. I now had to swallow, after everything else that I had gone through, now I have herpes. Now give me a minute to dry my eyes so I can tell you what I know now.

Dear Sis,

I know that God really loves me. It could have been HIV. Some of you reading this do have HIV and maybe even full blown AIDS. And I am so very sorry for that. I really wish that didn't happen to you. I promise I do. But I know now that I should have turned away from him before I ever turned to him. It is foolish to think that you are ready for another relationship right after you get out of one. You are not ready at all. You need to allow time for God to love on you through a relationship with Jesus. Jesus is the best friend, lover, and husband you can ever have. I know that sounds strange but as you will read just to cry out to Jesus is help. He will comfort you and take the loneliness away.

If you have a disease then all I can say is take your medicine and do as the doctors instruct and never give up hope. God can cure you if it is in His will. I am a witness. If it is not in His will to cure you then it is His purpose that it gives Him glory through your life somehow. I know that Nicolas should have never had time to spend with me after that. Even though he used slick conversation with me much like satan did Eve, I should have turned away. I asked God to forgive me for ever giving him a listening ear. I will say this. Please know that you cannot go far enough for God to not be willing to reach down and save you. He is never surprised at our choices, we are. God is so willing to save you and love you and cleanse you. God bless your hearts.

Isaiah 38:17-20 King James Version

Behold, for peace I had great bitterness: but thou hast in love to my soul delivered it from the pit of corruption: for thou hast cast all my sins behind thy back. For the grave cannot praise thee, death cannot celebrate thee: they that go down into the pit cannot hope for thy truth. The living, the living, he shall praise thee, as I do this day: the father to the children shall make known thy truth. The LORD was ready to save me: therefore we will sing my songs to the stringed instruments all the days of our life in the house of the LORD.

Chapter 15 – The Assembly of the Saints

That was one heck of a story, right? I tell you and it is all true. Well at this point in my life I had been working at that job I mentioned before. I was completely not happy but I did make a couple of lifelong friends out of the deal. One was Robert Matthew Johnson. That is a real name. We would get to work about an hour to an hour and a half before our bosses arrived. We did our work so fast we usually were twiddling our thumbs in the wait for them to get to the office and give us more work. Sometimes we would take documents that were in use that was old and used and re-create them on the computer for a cleaner look. One morning my life changed for the better. I suppose it was God shining love on me again.

Matt (his nickname) came to work with a small keyboard. Now the last keyboard I had was stolen from me. My former husband had let a guy live with us for a while and one day we came home and he was gone and so was the keyboard that my dad got me. All the time I was in the University and broke, I never pawned my musical instruments because I am a musical instrument and those items meant a great deal to me. At any rate, this particular morning Matt put the keyboard right in front of me. I looked down like I was looking at an alien. It had been so long since my hands touched anything musical I was almost scared. This is the feeling that a lot of people experience when the thought of touching or reaching for something you once dreamed comes to them. Maybe you have a dream of finishing school or starting a business. It could be anything. Maybe a dream of speaking to someone you had not spoken to for years presents itself. But instead of touching it or reaching for it, we run and hide in fear. God says that we do not have to be afraid of sudden fear when it comes because the Lord is our confidence and he will keep our foot from being taken. (Proverbs 3:25-26) Trust me I understand though. The thought of such can be so clinching.

We turned on the keyboard and I put my hands on the keys. It felt like I was going in slow motion. I realized that I had not really sang or played the entire time with my former husband. I just stood there and began to cry and I could not stop. Matt just stood there all loving. He was only 18 years old at the time. This was his first job so he not lived any kind of life to really understand what I was going through. He just stood there with his loving self and let me gather my emotions together. Turns out he is quite the musician himself. He plays the piano, sax, sings and the guitar. I began to play a song that I wrote when I was 15. I started playing and played through the whole song! I was so delighted. For a moment I felt like I was still myself. Myself. I realized that I forgot who that was. At that moment I prayed that God would let my life get better and better every year. I prayed that I could look back and say that this year was better than last year. We lost track of time and we had to scramble to get ourselves together for our bosses.

That afternoon at work Christina came by the office. She was the young lady who had the position that I currently worked in. She had been inviting me to her church since the day I came in to interview for the job. It was now July and hot! I decided that day that I did want to go to the church she invited me to. So I went. That Sunday morning was one of those cool summer mornings and we got to church on time and I was ready for change. That preacher got up with a smile and began to preach. The choir was so awesome. The music was incredible and I know good music. This man was so sweet but when he began preaching something happened about halfway through. It was like fire had taken over him and he was roaring through his message. I started crying because I felt like I had sinned so badly and I knew it anyway. I was co convicted and trapped in realness. My heart was pounding. I remember him saying, "This is the God that has given you life and protected you and you are still going around like a whore!!!" He said that with that black long figure pointed right at me. I know he wasn't pointing at me because he didn't know me, but God did. God was right. When he finished and there was an altar call I knew that I needed to go up there. An altar call is when there is a moment set aside in a church service so that those who had not come to know Jesus Christ as their personal Lord and Savior can come up and make that declaration. The altar can also be used for other reasons, but that is the main one.

I was so scared I whispered in Christina's ear, "I wanna go up there." And she replied to me, "Well go!" I said, "I'm scare will you hold my hand?" She quickly took my hand and we went up. I was crying so badly and I was so embarrassed. I wasn't too worried about the people. I was embarrassed at my own self. I met the Lord for my own self that morning and decided to join Spirit of Life

Ministries. The pastor came to me and told me I such purpose on my life and that God loves me and I am special to Him. It was like hearing Japanese. I don't speak a word of that language. Smile. I did hear him though.

That week at work my co-worker invited me to go to her house for lunch. I declined. Everyone came back high or drunk. A day later at lunch when our bosses were out we went in the back of the building. My co-worker rolled a joint and asked me to join in. I went to the back with her. One person took their turn, then another, and then it was my turn. I had the joint up to my lips and it was so close and I was ready to take my puff but something happened. I heard in my head, "This is not you anymore and you don't need this. You want to go forward not backwards and you want next year to be better than this year." I pulled my hand back and then down. I handed the joint back and said, "This is not me anymore and I don't want to go backwards so please don't invite me into this anymore. Love ya though." With a smile, I turned and walked back into the office. I went to the bathroom and washed my face and hands. I looked up and smiled. It had been years since I could look in the mirror and smile. I was really scared but I did feel a bit confident because now I had God in my life for real.

Dear Sis,

I know that God used Christina to pull me into Spirit of Life Ministries where a Pastor by the name of Jerome Nelson, Sr. would be waiting to preach and uncompromising word to me. It was all God though because we can only call ourselves blessed to be used by the Holy Spirit. For the word says that it is not by His might but by His spirit does He draw us. He was used to remind me that God had not forgotten about me and that He still loved me. Even after all I had done. I know that Matt was used to remind me that the gifts and talents that God places in you, no one and no thing can ever pull them out of you.

I am so thankful that the Holy Spirit gave me the power to walk away from an 8 yearlong addiction to marijuana. I never went back after that moment. Even though I was offered it and was around it after that, I never went back. All glory goes to God for that one. Oh God thank you so much for empowering me to walk away from that which could have had me bound even today. Thank you Jesus. God did it for me and he can do it for you too. I know that Pastor Nelson was so meant to be my Shepherd and I thank God that he is still my Pastor now.

Jeremiah 3:14-15 King James Version

"Return oh backsliding children ", says the Lord, "for I am married to you. I will take you, one from a city and two from a family, and I will bring you to Zion. And I will give you Shepherds according to my heart, who will feed you with knowledge and understanding."

Chapter 16 — Never Go Back After Freedom

By the year of 2004, I had been ignorant enough to start communicating on a chat line. I forgot how I came upon that thing but it was a mistake and it catered to lonely and depressed women; whom would be found by horny and out-of-control men. Of course, that only depresses a person further because nothing good at all comes from those chat lines. I had been attending SLM (Spirit of Life Ministries) pretty regularly. Every time I would go I would receive more encouragement and chastisement from the Lord. This was really good. You can sit under such a strong word and still not have the heart and courage to reach up and grab the blessing. Sometimes God is truly waiting for us to move in Wisdom.

Loneliness is a booger-bear. Really, the lack of the love of Jesus Christ is a booger-bear. See when you receive that, loneliness and selfish emotions will flee. The love of Jesus will fill you up and make you whole like never before. Well, I decided I would call the chat line and give it a try. I ended up talking to one guy and we exchanged numbers. We talked for about 3 weeks and I agreed with him that it was time for us to meet. It was always hard for me to get a baby sitter so I didn't ask unless it was a severe request. I allowed this stranger to come to my apartment. My children were sleep and to make the story short, I engaged in sexual intercourse with him. I have to be honest here and say that no protection was used. We started and about 5 seconds later the man released inside of me. I am not exaggerating either. It took 5 seconds for the devil to make me feel stupid again.

Two weeks later I found out that I was pregnant and I called this man and told him that I was pregnant. I remember exactly what this man said to me. This is the same man who told me he was just looking for someone special in his life and he was tired of trying and hoped that he could just settle down. When he met me he told me how beautiful I was and he couldn't believe I was on the chat line. Anyway, the man said, "What!? Are you some kinda trick or hoe! You full of games. You gave it to me so quick I just knew you were on the pill. You must need some money or something because you have the damn kids. Don't call me no more!" And with that, he hung up in my face. I didn't even know this man's last name. Well. That's it. I called from different numbers for about 3 days when I realized I was in it by myself. I borrowed some money from a few people and I went to the clinic and had an abortion. Sin begets sin begets sin begets sin begets death and destruction and separation from God. I guess the truth is I have not received God's forgiveness for this because I am here crying again. I know that I am covered in the blood of Christ. Please attach your heart to my plea. RAISE YOUR STANDARDS TO JESUS SO THIS WILL NOT HAPPEN TO YOU. When I finish this chapter I will receive this area of forgiveness for myself though trust me. I went to church and I wrote on a piece of paper and handed it to Christina what I had done. And she wrote back that there is no condemnation to those that are in Jesus Christ. That loved me.

That summer my former husband had gotten released from prison and I asked God if I should give him another chance and if jail can really reform a person. God told me to read Psalm 27 and memorize it. I did that. I tried the pure walk for a while and therefore was able to start hearing from God. When he arrived at my apartment the children were so happy to see him. When he walked in I saw a huge N-O all over his body. He never understood why I didn't take him back. He made friends with the only people in the apartment complex that was trash. There were signs all over. So I kicked him out of my life again. He threatened me a few hours after he told me he loved me and couldn't live without me. I played the dumb roll and told him my parents were going to contact his parole officer to make sure he was ok because they had never heard of someone being released from prison and coming to another state and that was 'ok'. That's when he told me to tell my parents to "stay the F out of his business." He left and went back to his home state. God blessed me again with protection.

On to better days, my job had surprised me one morning and told me they were putting the entire office staff on part time. I was truly scared. I already didn't make enough money to afford my simple 2 bedroom apartment. I was blessed by God to get a job as an Assistant Manager/Leasing Agent at an apartment complex. It paid more and offered benefits. I decided I wanted better for my life and for my children. So I went to the junior college of my choice. I was so nervous and scared. I felt embarrassed and prayed I didn't run into anyone I knew.

The devil fought me like a men hound getting into school. Finally, my pell grant application went through and that would pay for school and my books.

However, it was held up for some reasons. I prayed and asked God to please help me better myself. Allow me to do better please. My brother told me he would give me the down payment to start classes. I had the money to buy that overpriced government book. So I was in school. I was never any good at school except for music and drama classes. History and government were my very worst classes. God set it up that this class was the only one available that was conducive to my schedule. My mother watched the kids for me on the day of class. That was amazing because I had been such a disappointment she probably had no desire to help me due to my track record. You reap what you sow.

I passed my class with a B. I had to work so hard and study so much and put up with a very arrogant professor that was truly lifted up in pride. I didn't care though because I thought it was funny that he was so entertained by himself. I signed up for the next semester and this time I signed up for 2 classes. The enemy fought again and made it hard for the financial aid to manifest. By this time the lady over my account was looking for the issues and let me in school anyway because she knew the money would come through eventually. That was another hurdle jumped. Thank you Jesus of Nazareth.

Dear Sis,

I know that God really did bless me because that time it could have been AIDS that got me. I give God all the glory for his protection. I asked God to protect him too and to this day I have nothing against that man. It amazes me how easy it is for a man to walk away from his child. I have sense given my two aborted children a funeral and cried out to the Lord for forgiveness. It took a while for me to completely received God's forgiveness in that area. I will not pretend to be over that completely. Honestly it is something I am still walking through. I don't think about it every day, but I do hurt to know that I not only put myself in these predicaments but I made the choice of abortion. I don't know how to tell you to get over it all I can say is receive healing in that area. Just like Christina wrote, God is such a loving and gracious God. There is now no condemnation to those who are in Christ Jesus (Romans 8:1). However, please make a note. The bible also says that we should not frustrate the grace of God (Galatians 2:21 KJV). So choose wisely.

I know that I should not have given my former a chance. In my life I believe if God takes it away, trust Him. God knows what He is doing. Do fight His directions. God told me if I keep my mouth off of my former that he would keep him away from us as long as he walked in that spirit of destruction. I did my part and God continues to do His part. Glory to God.

I thank God for my brother allowing himself to be used in my life so wonderfully. He too could have said no because of my track record. But God's track record is all that counts and I thank Him for looking at the heart of a man.

1 Samuel 16:7 NIV Version

But the LORD said to Samuel, "Do not consider his appearance or his height, for I have rejected him. The LORD does not look at the things man looks at. Man looks at the outward appearance, but the LORD looks at the heart."

Chapter 17 – My First Taste at Purpose

I was blessed to develop some very great acquaintances at the job. I met a family and we became good friends and still are today. The mother of the family starred in my first play. One of the other residences I moved in were two guys. One of them introduced me to a guy who worked with me to write my first play. I gave the guy all of the information and directed him how I saw the play progresses. As a result of my ideas and his awesome writing, I had a play. I really stepped out on faith with that. Man, are you talking about a lot of hard work! This was the year 2005. Now I am here about to kiss destiny. During this time, I was so busy with school, work and the kids that I wasn't so badly distracted with men. When you are pressing for Jesus and walking in your purpose you have less time to be distracted. However, I was still in love with Nicolas – or in lust. I did believe I loved him at the time. I had met another guy on the chat line in the fall of that year. I agree with you if you are saying, "What? She didn't have enough?" Let me tell you something and you may hear me say this over and over again. You never know how far God will have to let a person go in their mess in order to get their attention for a true turn around.

I remember meeting Shawn and he came to meet me at my job when I was there on a Saturday. That was so out of order. I could have lost my job on a man. Anyway, I just couldn't see this man was about game. I recently had a conversation with a man of God that said he wrote his cd to women. He did this so that he could talk to them and encourage them. At the same time, he said he also challenged them with some rebuke. I told him I wish more men of God would do that. Because if women who were clueless about game, like I was, could hear the voice of an honest man of God we would be able to notice game and stay away from it. Moving on though, this guy Shawn seemed to be all that. He was handsome and seemed to have an education. I remember one day asking him why we never talked on the phone at night. He said that he got off earlier than me and that he went to bed early.

He would call me all the time during the day. We emailed each other and chatted on instant messenger. I would receive all kinds of cute cards and encouragement. He told me about his church and gave me the name. Because the church did exist, I figured I could trust him. I have said this before but this is a perfect time to say it again. Beware of fine devils. Also, the closer you get to God, the further Satan will reach into his trick bag to ensnare you. Please believe that. Well, I did end up having sex and sinning with him. It was unprotected so I was nervous about getting pregnant. I told him I was worried and of course the courting and

About two weeks later, I had met another guy on the chat line to bounce back. One evening I received a phone call from a woman with the nicest voice on the other end. She said, "I am not trying to be mean to you or cause you trouble but I have some questions for you and I would like you to answer them for me. I have a cell phone bill in front of me and I want to read a number to you. Can you tell me who that is to you?" I told her yes and she read off the number. I told her that was Shawn and we were seeing each other. She said, "Let me close my door because I don't want my kids to hear this." At that moment I knew that this was a call that I had made many times when I was married. Shawn told me he wasn't with anyone and he didn't have any kids. I could see that vampire telling me he didn't have a woman, but to deny his kids really hurt me and pissed me off. Now I was on the other end of the conversation that I had been so many times before that I don't even want to count them.

I told her that he told me he wasn't married and didn't have kids. I told her that I would never communicate with him again and that I was so very sorry for being a part of this. I told her about my first marriage. I encouraged her that if she still loves her husband not to leave and see if they can get counseling to get past this and stay together for their children and for each other. I even told her about my marriage. I told her not to give up just because he betrayed her because God could change anybody. She asked me if God had changed my former. No. I said however that was him and there is a difference. I prayed for her. I covered her heart and her children. I prayed for him. I cried with her. I can't completely explain just how devastated I was because I completely understood how she felt but I never wanted to inflict that pain on another woman. But I did. Because I was being over-much-wicked (Ecclesiastes 7:17), I caused myself to walk into a trap that not only hurt me but children and their mother and most of all, the sacred covenant of marriage. We never spoke again. That night I went to bed crying and I couldn't even pray. I knew I was wrong. So I, as so many times before, desperately bounced into another potentially destructive relationship.

All the time this was happening, I was still going to church and getting whipped by the word coming forth from Pastor Nelson. In November 2005 I was at practice and Nicolas called and said, "You know I have been thinking about your beautiful eyes. Have you gotten into a relationship yet? You know I miss you." I ate that up so easy and so quick. I really still loved this guy and wished so badly that he would just marry me. I was comparing him to the other vampires I was dating and said to myself, "Nicolas never did this stuff. He really doesn't have another woman. And I know about his kids. I need to be there for him so that he can choose me." So I let him come to visit me. Or should I say, I let him come to screw me again. I hope that wasn't to 'strong' of language for the saints. It is real though. It is the truth anyway. As quick as he came to visit was as quick as he left.

So the other guy I mentioned that I was dating was trying to get close to me. Because I was living in an apartment I didn't have anywhere to hide my baby's Christmas presents, so I kept them in my trunk. One day I was hanging out with him and he saw the presents. He said to me, "You must have it going on." I told him it is hard to raise two children on my own. I struggled all the time and paid on bills. I never had the money to pay all my living expenses except at tax return time. So this guy decided he was going to ask me for some money to help him pay his rent. That really got my attention. I was thinking, "I know this punk did not ask me for money and he sees me struggling with my two kids. I don't get child support. I have to drag my babies everywhere with me. I don't ever get a break. There is no one in my life saying just let me keep them so you can have a weekend to yourself. I love my babies but everyone needs 'me' time. I am in school. I stay up all night studying and on the weekends rehearsing a play. Before he even offered to help me with something, he is going to take something? Sike!" I told him I am not able to help you with that and don't ever, ever, ever call me again.

I meant that. He did call me but I repeated myself. I was now determined to pay attention to my Pastor and walk in purity. This means I was going to stop having sex and start developing my personal relationship with God so that I could be whole for the first time and restored. I cried out to God for Him to help me. I begged him to help me.

I had received a copy of my play from the guy who recorded it on DVD. I gave it to my Pastor and asked him to watch it. I wasn't committed to my church at that time. I was just attending. This play had cursing in it. My whole point was to take this character and show how you should stop. But you can't make a point to the world using the world's ways. I remember talking to my Pastor's wife, Ms. B. (she is a pastor as well) and she told me she couldn't even read past the first page. I was a tad hurt. I wanted to understand why and when I pray God shows me it was because of the cursing. I talked to her about it and she explained just that. She said you could have found a way to make the point without actually cursing. The play was a total success!

It was now January of 2006. I had left the chat lines alone for good. I had begun to walk in a type of courage because I had not been conversing with men. My boss had begun to walk in a huge sense of envy towards me due to the play going forth and some of her residences having been involved in the play. She began to be very ugly to me. I was taught that our bosses were our authority and we were to handle them with honor. (Hebrews 13:17) Now not everyone who is in leadership will walk worthy of this calling but you are not responsible for their behavior but for your own behavior and accountability to God the Father. In the fall of 2005 I would leave my job for a 2 hour approved lunch break. The office was very slow at that time. I would come back and work and extra hour at the end of the day so that I could make up that hour. When 2006 came along I needed to have the same schedule for my last semester of music theory. If I did not take the class then, I wouldn't graduate until 2008! So I prayed for 30 days straight because my boss told me she would not approve that again. She had been telling our head boss that I was never there and I left her alone all day. She told him so many lies he would have believed I was from Scotland! I was producing well in my job too. I rented just about everyone that walked into that apartment complex. I had a 98% rent history and 75% of the people I rented to stayed and paid rent on time.

One Sunday my Pastor's, pastor over him, came and preached the word. She went right into my area and confirmed my prayers and God gave me my answer. He told me that He was my provision and to trust Him. So I turned in my resignation. I was so scared but God wanted to teach me about stepping out on faith. You are talking about scared out of my mind! I have two babies and no financial support other than my job. But I wanted to trust God and I was tired of having so much to offer a job and getting paid hardly anything. I felt that if I didn't finish school I would never be able to increase my salary potential. And besides all of that, I am a musician and a teacher and I needed to be doing that and getting paid for it. Know this. Shortly after I left, the apartment complex was sold and everybody had to find another job. Know that when you are walking with Jesus, you are walking with the covering of the Holy Spirit. When you leave, that anointing leaves.

It was February 2006 and it was getting very tight financially. I was on the hunt for a job 8 hours a day and couldn't find someone that would hire me and allow me to finish school. I received a call on one of the days I should have been counting on God only for attention. It was Nicolas. I remember what he said like it was yesterday. He said, "Hey girl, are you still looking for your husband." That's it sisters. I was still so desperate for a husband, which is all it took to get my attention again. I tell you, a vampire can spot its prey very easily. Why? Because they are constantly on the hunt. They are good at what they do. I let him come over. The first night I put him on the couch thinking that was the right thing to do. I should have never invited him in. I was proud of myself for being strong that night. I was still determined to walk in purity. I really wanted it. But I really wanted a husband too. The next day when the kids were at school we were sitting on the sofa talking. Never forget that the devil is very patient and will play along with your game until he gets what he wants from you. Which is to suck you dry and leave you for dead.

I fell flat on my face with this man AGAIN. When it was over, mind you I did not even reach my satisfaction in the sin, (in other words no climax) he went to the bathroom. When he came back in the room I asked him if we could take a nap together and would he just hold me. Anytime you have to ask a man to hold you, girl he is NOT the one. He didn't. As a matter of fact, he told me that it wasn't necessary for him to do that for me to get comfortable. He said he should not have been with me like that. He always said that. Every time I let him in he would tell me he should not have done that and he was upset that we went there. As if to say that he knew he shouldn't because of God or because he knew he wasn't ready to commit to me. So I got a tad pissed off. I asked him why he would come over here and why would he ask me if I was looking for my husband if he knew he just wanted to have sex with me. I cried. I asked him why he would do this to me over and over again knowing that I loved him and he had no intentions of being with me seriously. Do you know that thing said to me? He said, "What have I ever said or done Vawn, that makes you think or gave you the impression that I wanted something serious?" Now check this out. In all honesty, he wasn't completely saying that to be hateful, he really said that to make me think about the reality. Remember what I said about reality a while back?

What happens is we, as women, imagine and daydream about what we want to happen; all the while, reality is a totally different place. So we dream and wish for what is happening to be what we are dreaming, so much so, that we stay in a terrible and destructive situation hoping that your dream will become a reality and it never ever happens. I truly pray that is clear. The devil will always tell on himself. So when Nicolas said that it was like I heard him. God uses all kinds of donkeys to speak to us. And that was the biggest donkey of them all. I sucked up my tears and smiled. I kissed him on the cheek and said bye. I didn't say leave. I didn't say anything but bye. When it's over, it is over. Hear this and head. When you see the light, stop cold turkey. Here it is again. YOU DON'T OWE HIM NOTHING. NOTHING AT ALL. NOT A CONVERSATION. NOT AN EXPLANATION. NOTHING AT ALL. NOT EVEN THE BREATH THAT SAYS PLEASE LEAVE OR I WANT YOU TO GO OR GIVE ME MY 'WHATEVER' BACK. JUST 'BYE'. Let him figure it out. Kind of like you had to take forever to figure out he was a vampire. Yeah. Just walk away. The security in that is if you start talking you may get ensnared again. When he left I went to my computer and emailed him to never ever communicate with me again. I wrote for him not even to respond if he gets a message from me. I erased his numbers from my phone and I didn't have them memorized. I hated that I did that right after because I still loved him. But I did it. Then I cried for hours.

That night I went to church and my pastor preached a message called "Living with and Accountability to God in Mind." Jesus of Nazareth. I was so gripped with conviction already because I had fallen when I really wanted to get it right this time. I was nervous about going to church because I didn't want my Pastor to smell it on me. In that message, he called my name 3 times. Once while he was explaining how a man should court you and treat you on a date. He talked about purity. He then came to me and prophesied that I don't need a man around me that will codependent and fixated on me. He said that I need to have a man that will court me through the word of God and one that will have a long distance relationship with me through the word. He also called me out to get up and show how a man should pull the chair out for you. He was all in my house and reading me up and down. I cried so hard. I wasn't worried about people seeing me because I was ready to stop living like that and being used and thrown away. The pastor said that Jesus could be the best husband, friend, and comforter for me and show me that I don't need a man to live in joy. I went to the altar for prayer.

After church, I was so convicted I had to confess to someone. I found a friend of mine. He is such a wonderful man. At that time I didn't know him that well. I looked at him and started crying and told him that I fell and I was so ashamed. He squared me off in front of him and looked me in my eyes and encouraged me. He told me that he had the past and a testimony too. He said that we all fall but that doesn't separate us from God's love for us. We can get up and try again and be healed. That was so loving and encouraging. See I had just gotten the chastisement side of God, which is real, but God loves me so much He gave me the sweet and graceful side of Him as well. I went home knowing that was the last time Nicolas would ever be in my life and happy about it and that was the last time any man would be with me sexually until my husband found me. See the change? First I was looking for a husband and now I was lining up to God's way which is the man finding you.

Dear Sis,

I know that God put Pastor Nelson in my life for purpose as my Shepherd. I know that when you are a single woman and you live by yourself that you should not even let a man inside your home. At all. You just shouldn't trust me. There has to come a time when you draw the line and stand so far back you can't see the line anymore. Some say stand 10 feet back. I needed to stand so far back that I couldn't see the line. In other words, I just needed to draw the line and turn and walk away.

I know that I did well by ministering to that woman and encouraging her to stay with her family. However, I should have never been there. My Pastor had been preaching to me for 3 years and I had plenty of time to hear God before then. I was blessed by God's grace in that situation.

I know that vampires will suck you dry and leave you for dead. They don't care about anything but their own agenda. If you show them your cards first, which most weak women do, they will use that knowledge to help them overpower you. It is important to set your standards according to Christ's ways only.

MIRROR MOMENT: To keep doing something the same way and expecting a different result is called insanity. So this is what I did and this is what I highly encourage you to do right now. Get to a mirror. Pray that the Lord God will be with you as you confront and confess the innermost things that hurt you. I confessed my acts of fornication, abortion, addictions, being overweight, not gaining my degree, insecurities and everything I did not like about myself. Some of those things God spoke to me and told me where I needed to love myself and He ultimately granted healing in those areas. That healing was – is - a process but it happened. Sometimes when we are able to 'cry out' to the Lord we can begin the healing process. This is why I strongly encourage you to have a mirror moment.

James 1:22-25

21 So get rid of all uncleanness and the rampant outgrowth of wickedness, and in a humble (gentle, modest) spirit receive and welcome the Word which implanted and rooted [in your hearts] contains the power to save your souls. 22 But be doers of the Word [obey the message], and not merely listeners to it, betraying yourselves [into deception by reasoning contrary to the Truth]. 23 For if anyone only listens to the Word without obeying it and being a doer of it, he is like a man who looks carefully at his [own] natural face in a mirror; 24 For he thoughtfully observes himself, and then goes off and promptly forgets what he was like. 25 But he who looks carefully into the faultless law, the [law] of liberty, and is faithful to it and perseveres in looking into it, being not a heedless listener who forgets but an active doer [who obeys], he shall be blessed in his doing (his life of obedience).

1 Corinthian 6:13-20 King James Version

13 Meats for the belly, and the belly for meats: but God shall destroy both it and them. Now the body is not for fornication, but for the Lord; and the Lord for the body. 14 And God hath both raised up the Lord, and will also raise up us by his own power. 15 Know ye not that your bodies are the members of Christ? shall I then take the members of Christ, and make them the members of an harlot? God forbid. 16 What? know ye not that he which is joined to an harlot is one body? for two, saith he, shall be one flesh. 17 But he that is joined unto the Lord is one spirit. 18 Flee fornication. Every sin that a man doeth is without the body; but he that committeth fornication sinneth against his own body. 19What? know ye not that your body is the temple of the Holy Ghost which is in you, which ye have of God, and ye are not your own? 20For ye are bought with a price: therefore glorify God in your body, and in your spirit, which are God's.

Chapter 18 – The Turn Around

I decided to make an appointment with my Pastor B. She made room in her schedule for me and I went to visit. I was blessed to spend almost 2 uninterrupted hours with her. During our meeting, I must have said something to her for her to suggest a book to me. The name of the book is, *"Adult Children of Alcoholics"* by Janet Geringer Woititz. This is a very thin book. I love to read books so it doesn't take me long to read through a novel. It took me 5 months to finish this book. I remember reading the first couple of pages and falling on the floor literally on my face and crying hard. I could not believe that a woman that knows nothing about me could know so much about me. I had to pray before I picked up the book to read more because I knew it would be telling me more about myself. What I learned was a lot of what I saw attractive in men was from my own father. I learned that a lot of why I chose the men that I did was based on what I saw in him. I learned that a lot of what happened in my relationships was based on what happened between my father and me and my father and my mother. Oh, my Lord, it is about to get deep.

I always cried out to God, "Why is when they know I love them they push me away?" I couldn't see that I was clinging on to men for dear life. I should have been clinging on to God alone. But what happened with having a parent that was an alcoholic is we get a false impression of what love is and should be. See the alcoholic comes home and loves you but is drunk silly. So you go up to them as a child to get a hug or some love and the parent says, "Not now." They say that because they are drunk and you walk away with your feelings hurt. Now, when it is time to bring them the aspirin, you again feel loved because now you are needed. In my case, it was in the morning. I would bring my dad 2 pieces of toasted bread. I would toast the bread and then put butter on it. Then I would put it in the microwave for few seconds to melt the butter. He loved it so much that he would tell me it was perfect every time I brought it to him. I felt so important that I was the only 'one' that could help my daddy feel better. I took pride in bringing him those 2 slices of bread. Then he was ready to hug me and love on me. See the problem? See the pattern. So I grew up seeking men that had issues that only 'I' could help them with. So I wasn't attracted to a complete man.

No. I needed to be with someone that had issues so that I could 'help them'. Detrimental with a capitol 'D'.

The other side of that was my dad would come home drunk sometimes from the club and would bring food with him. He would always share. I looked forward to eating at 12 or 1 in the morning to spend time with him. We would watch musicals and sing to them and get full. I enjoyed that time with him. I am grateful for all he taught me musically and I love him. I have to be honest and say that I am not enjoying sharing this but I will because God called me to do so. So what this taught me was to eat as much as I wanted when I was feeling bad. It also taught me that it was ok to be drunk or inebriated when performing or enjoying music. It was so possible that I would grow up and get hooked on weed. I would feel like I couldn't listen to music or perform without being high on weed or drunk. My daddy is as human as the next man or woman bless his heart. He never talked to me crazy though. I was his princess. He did, however, talk to my mother crazy and I heard a lot of it. I saw a lot of it. I found some terrible things that they don't even know I know about. Still to this day even. It all affected my decision-making process in a being with a man.

It was time for me to come real with myself. I didn't know what a good man was because I never saw the response from a woman being treated well for my own eyes. I never knew how to treat a man because I never saw a woman treat a man well either. It is the truth anyway. Lord Jesus. My mom never fixed my dad his dinner. I don't even remember them smiling at each other. I never heard my mother encourage my dad. I remember one time when I was about 15, my brother was gone to college, my mom and dad had an argument. He was so depressed and she was so depressed because God was not the glue that was holding them together that he went and got his gun and was shouting he would kill himself. My mother sat on the sofa and just shrugged her shoulders because she was tired of his abuse. He was tired of no love. I ran after my dad and held his arm and begged him not to kill himself. He was crying and said that he couldn't do it anymore and he was nothing. The church we went to offered absolutely nothing on the encouragement and love of Jesus Christ, which is so detrimental because God is love. So if you are a church and you are not teaching that revelation, you are not teaching. It is the truth anyway. My daddy dropped the gun and I took it and placed it in front of my mom. I had the nerve to be mad at her for not caring to stop him so I said something to her. She said, "Girl your daddy don't have the nuts to kill himself." I walked into my room and cried hard. I was so confused. I knew my dad cheated on her or at least I had heard about it. He was mean to her too. But then I knew my mom hated my dad and she had zero passion for him understandably so. I realized that all the time my brother fought me made me comfortable with having to fight a man for love. I realized that hearing all the abusive words from my brother made me comfortable with allowing a man abuse me verbally. What to do?

I decided I would create a standard for any man who wanted to date me. I also decided I would draw closer to my Pastor B so that I could learn how to be a godly woman and be a godly wife. I thought this part of the book would be easier to write because this is the turnaround period. But I was wrong. It isn't easy telling a true story when it isn't funny or happy. I am praying that it will bless somebody. I am not made at my family nor do I blame them for anything. It was truly the purpose of God to allow this misery to turn into ministry. By telling this story I pray somebody will think about what they are doing and choose God completely and His ways above all other ways like their life depends on it. Because it truly does. Glory to God.

So my standard was now Jesus. My examples were now Jerome and Betty Nelson. I began to watch carefully and come to church more often. I was also ready to serve in the choir with integrity. My standard was this:

1. Love God with all his heart and be submitted under a pastor with the same Holy Spirit teaching. (Which is only one true Holy Spirit teaching)
2. Love himself as God would have him as a complete man.
3. Have a true love and appreciation for family.
4. Be goal driven and creative.
5. Have a natural romantic side to court me forever.

My standard for myself was the same. When I finished the book, 'Adult Children of Alcoholics,' I had begun a true walk of healing from within and forgiveness for all.

There was a test to come quickly. I still didn't have a job. I had been temping at an apartment complex and they were going to offer me the job but I had an anxiety attack. When I got out of the hospital my mechanic called me and told me that my car was dead. He said that he could fix it but if I could it would be better for me to get a new car. Right before I had that call, I received and offer for another apartment complex. I was so happy that I finally had a job. Then I get the call that I can't get to work. (Smile) I told God, "You told me you would be my provision and to trust you. I have been walking in purity as you said, so please help me." When I got home I had a $1000 check in the mail. It was a grant that I had applied to receive and God did it! So I called my dad and asked him if he would take me to look for a car the next weekend. He said yes. I had to get a ride to work that week but that was ok.

My dad showed up and blew my mind because he brought $500 dollars with him to help me get a car. That was God trust me. He took me around and we went to one dealership that had an angel there. We didn't get anywhere completely so went looking at other places. The angel called me and said please give us a chance to work the deal. So we came back and they handed me keys to a car to drive off the lot. I didn't understand what was happening. I hadn't given them any money and they didn't ask for any. But I drove off the lot with an SUV that I wanted. I couldn't sleep that night and I called the Angel the next morning and told him I couldn't afford a truck. So I went back and got a car. I hated that because I wanted that truck but I knew I couldn't afford the gas, the insurance or a tire if it busted. He was impressed because he told me most folks in my financial situation always come in demanding vehicles they know they can't afford. I then told him the truth about my job. I had first lied and said that I had been on my job for 6 months. I told him if God can't make it happen with the truth then I would go get another car from a 'mom and pop' place. He encouraged me and said he would work on it.

Six weeks later, still driving a loaner car, my angel came to my job and dropped off my new car and gave me a hug and said that I had blessed him. I gave God glory right there! Thank you, Jesus. Then I got home and had an eviction notice on my door. (Smile) I said ok God. What is the deal? I ended up applying for financial help from the church and they helped me get caught up again. Glory to God. Now comes the test. Remember this guy from college that I loved so much? The one that just knew me? Well while on a dating website that dude found me. He called me. I am not sure how he got my number but he did. It was Shelton from chapter 5. I really never got to say goodbye to him. After he reminded me who he was I was delighted. I will make this story as short as I can.

I was so drawn to him because he knew how to talk to me. He was still so encouraging with my music. I caught him up on my endeavors and he thought that was awesome. We re-kindled our friendship and I looked forward to him calling.

One day he called me and let me know he was going to be home for two weeks. He was married and I was falling in love with a married man. I had excused it because he was mine first anyway. I knew I was wrong but I was lonely. We were not touching each other; we were just talking on the phone. Remember when I said that the devil is patient?, First he gets your toe caught, then your foot, then your leg and then your whole body falls in. By that time it is so hard to get out. Well Shelton called me and told me he was coming to town. I let him come to visit me when the kids went to sleep. At least I thought they were sleep. Shelton got close to me and wanted to have sex. I did too. But I told him I didn't want that on me. I was walking in purity and he could never give me what I wanted. What happened to my list of standards? That went right out the door when lust came in!

All of a sudden I heard my daughter's voice. No kidding. I was so nervous. I went into the room and my daughter said to me, "I don't want you to have sex with him!" That little prophetess was 5 years old. God will always give you a way out. I asked him to leave. I discontinued communication with him at that time. Whew!

So now it was time for my daughter to start Kindergarten. I was so proud and nervous. I didn't have any money to buy her new clothes. I asked God to at least allow me to put new tennis shoes on her feet. I had $40 to last me for two weeks and I spent $20 on some new shoes for her. When I got to day care to pick them up there was a bag full of brand new clothes waiting for me! Beautiful clothes. There were panties, under shirts, socks, pants, shorts, and skirts. So cute I would not know how to shop for that stuff if I had the money. Then there was another bag full of shoes. I had so much stuff I had to go home and clean out her drawers and give everything away! God is the God of overflow. I wasn't able to keep my apartment but God did allow me to finish my lease. I was blessed with the chance to move back into my mother's house with her husband. Walking in purity opens God's hands to pour out blessings!

That Christmas I was still trying to catch up and I had no money to buy presents. One day at work my children's doctor office called and said they had a surprise for me. They said that the local fire department always calls them for them to choose 2 children from their patient census to buy toys for Christmas. They choose me! My very good friend and sister in the spirit went to pick up the toys. They gave me a huge bag (almost to my shoulders) full of toys, 2 bicycles, and 2 helmets! I was so touched because that year God showed me that He is faithful even in the things we just want. He keeps His promises and He IS my Jehovah Jireh, my God of provision. Glory to God.

I continued walking in purity and challenging every man that wanted to date me against the word of God and my standard list. None could get past number 2. In April of 2007, my car started acting up bad. My mother's car had broken down. That same mechanic said it may be time for a new car for my mother. We went to my angel at the car dealership for help. My mother got her a new car which was a hill to climb! Then the angel looked at me and said, "Do you remember when I said that if you keep your car payments up for a year you can get whatever car you wanted?" I shouted, "Yes!" He said, "Well choose." I chose the car of my choice that was on the lot.

The very next month which was about 2 weeks later, my mother and I went to the dealership and we signed papers on both of our cars. I walked away on a Friday, May 11, 2007, with my brand new car! The first my angle sold me was a 2002 and I bought it in 2006 so it was old. This time I got me a beautiful 2006 in 2007. That sounds like increase. Halleluiah! That is not all. That same evening I graduated with a 3.25 GPA from my college with an Associate Degree in Vocal Music Performance! I drove to my graduation in my new car with Matt. (Remember Matt?) It was so beautiful. Oh Lord God. Thank you for change and not giving up on me. Gratefulness is flowing from the heart.

Dear Sis,

As far as Shelton goes to commit sin starts in the mind. So I was sinning against God just talking to a married man on the phone. When God allows something to leave your life, leave it. God knows exactly what He is doing. Trust that.

I thank God that He and He alone gave me the strength to get to class and focus, then come home and study. All the while being mother. He allowed it all for purpose. My minister of music was trying to start drama ministry going at church and needed a story about somebody going to through situation after situation but continuing to stay encouraged in the Lord. I said, "I have an idea!" Smile

So I wrote the skit entitled, "Encourage Yourself." It was a real part of my life story. It blessed the body of Christ. Somebody was encouraged because I made it through my Christ Jesus hand of help. For that I can't help but give God glory for the testimony of His love in my life. Oh Jesus. I know that God will not let you fall. I don't care what the situation looks like. Jesus will snatch you out of the snares of hell so quick it will make your head spin. Then God loves you so much that He will give you more than you need and exactly what you need because He loves you so much. And when you continue to develop a relationship with God you can begin to call Him Daddy. He is just that close to you and you to Him. Oh He won't let you fail. But He will take your past failures and turn them into your present victories. He will take your sins and turn them into your testimony of how He brought you out. Your misery will become your ministry and the body of Christ in the process will be blessed and you will help someone not go through the same mess you went through. Glory to God the Father. Halleluiah.

Acts 20:24 King James Version

But none of these things move me, neither count I my life dear unto myself, so that I might finish my course with joy, and the ministry, which I have received of the Lord Jesus, to testify the gospel of the grace of God.

Chapter 19 – Getting Closer

The summer before I graduated someone gave me a really pivotal book entitled, "Knight in Shining Armor", by P.B. Wilson. That book changed my life as well. I was not able to afford to buy it so I was really blessed by God that he just 'put' it in my hands. This is a fairly thin book as well. I had to truly discipline myself to read it slowly. Because it was so right on time, that I wanted to fly through the book. Instead I took my time reading and learning.

I learned about waiting and allowing God to love you and create wholeness in you and you alone. I studied how wonderful singleness could truly be with just me and Jesus. There was no more drama. There were no more heart breaks. There was no more fornication. There were no more pitiful nights. I really received God's love for me and the most wonderful thing is I was able to look in the mirror and see beauty. I remember one Sunday church service when we were closing the service, my Pastor walked past me and picked me up in the spirit and said, "Vawn Gretta, all you have to stay pretty and keep walking this thing out and your man will find you."

By 2007 after I graduated, I was well on my way into more books to read to help me in my unmarried walk. Let me explain that. In the book that I just mentioned, the author suggests that you take six months to allow your reconstructing with God to be developed. While in that process she mentions 6 books that should be read. I will share those as well because they helped and me. I took her instructions seriously because I believed God 'put' this book in my hands so I should take what it said to be of the utmost importance. The first book was on fire! (They will be mentioned in order in the back) I learned about some really deep things concerning the mind, the church and heavenly places. The second, God dealt with me and money. Which is important as a help mate trust me! The third discovered un-forgiveness and how betrayal can really kill you.

That book was very important because her struggle had a lot to do with my struggle. She had some unresolved issues with her mother that caused her walk with her husband to be tremendously hindered. As far as loving my mother and not holding her responsible for anything that happened or did not happen to me in the past is no issue. When you hold somebody hostage for something that happened to you it's like having a rope around your own neck and pulling at it. Let's dig into these issues.

I really don't remember my mother saying something like this, "Baby come here and give mommy some sugar." I don't remember her pressing to give me a hug. I don't remember her telling me she loved me enough for me to remember she told me. I'm just being honest. But so that I don't bring that kind of long distance love into a local relationship I had to get before God about it. God and I had counseling sessions where I told him things that hurt my feelings. I will give you one example. When I was producing my first play, I would talk about it with my mother sometimes. She never really seemed that interested. On one particular day, I was, so excited about a break-through moment and wanted to share. She interrupted me by saying, "Vawn please stop. It just depresses me to hear you talking about that. You have children and you can barely take care of them and you are talking about putting a play together when you don't even have the money to pay off the theater. That is not how you do it. You are supposed to have something. Just stop." And I did just that. Not of course before I cried hard. She was correct in a sense; but, you see God will provide the necessary provisions for what He purposes. As we all know God brought all the finances needed for the work He gave me.

I did give my mother the very first ticket. She was in the front row and I watched her through the curtains when I wasn't on stage. She had such a pleased look on her face and I that made me smile. So I just choose to love my mother for where she was coming from because that is what pleases God. I don't walk in odds with her and I take her good days and her bad days and I love her the same. When she needs me I come running really fast. If you cannot love your parents with the God love and honor that He requires you will not function well in your relationship. I realize there are special situations to consider. But it is still a commandment to honor your father and mother so that your days will be long on earth. It is the same with my Father. I don't blame him for my poor choices with my past relationships. That will not profit anyone, anything. You need to love them with a God love.

With that said I began to notice I didn't tell my daughter or show her that I love her as much as I do. I asked her when I would fuss at her did she think I loved her and she said no.

So I would purpose to remind her I love her whenever I get on to her. Also in the morning, I created something called, 'cuddle time.' How this works is in the morning when I wake them up I just call their names and say it's time for cuddle time! Instead of 'get up and get ready for school' I say that and they come so sleepily and cute into my room. They both crawl into my bed and I hold them both and kiss them and tell them how much I love them. My son quickly falls asleep but my daughter scoots really close to me and I hold her extra tight. My son just loves the extra time to sleep! Smile. My daughter, however, cherishes this time. So I know that I didn't do a good job of showing her my love in the beginning and I really hate that. I wish I could go back and do it again with her. But I didn't have that with my mom so I didn't know I was doing it to my own baby. We will always have cuddle time.

By the end of that summer of 2007, I was really walking tight. There was this guy at my job that I fancied so much. He was so handsome and just fine y'all. Smile. One day I was trying to get out of my office with the quickness and I needed to help him first. He was filling out his paperwork and somehow we got into a conversation and I learned a big deal about him real quick. He was a man of God and he knew how to treat a woman. There were things that he was saying that I heard my Pastor say and things that I learned in having Jesus for a boyfriend. This is how I knew this man was awesome. So we became work friends. I soon found out that he was Jehovah Witness. I believe he was trying to convert me. Smile. I will be so honest and say I was really thinking about it. I considered if this man said all the right things before I knew he was of this faith and now that I know I don't think I should diss him.

Anyway, we would talk on the phone sometimes at night for hours and I enjoyed every minute of it. Mostly we were talking about God and what I knew and what he knew. What was so awesome is he was an evangelist to the heart. This guy was trained well. I knew some of the stuff he was saying wasn't quite on it with the revelation of the Spirit of the Lord, which is what is missing in that faith, (no offense) but I couldn't get the scripture out quick enough. So I was provoked to study the word of God more and more so that I could be ready to minister. I am smiling so hard. It's about time I get to a part of this book that I like. Cheese.

Check this out. So one day while walking in the sunshine of the Lord I check my email and guess who is coming to town? Nicolas. With my weak self, I responded to him and agreed to meet him at his hotel. I know you are choking. But it is true. You never know where you are until you are tested. I went to the hotel on July 4th. When I got there we went to his room and talked. Then that fine thing got close to me and kissed me and I let him. He started to touch me and I got turned completely on. I jumped up and was about to run out of there when he grabbed me and begged me to stay and not leave until I calmed down. He said that he was afraid that I would get hurt, driving. He apologized and then he told me how he appreciated me holding back on him. He told me that he just has a problem. He loves his wife and children but just loves women. He confided in me about another woman he had been seeing and I was laughing and crying in my spirit because I could have fallen with a man that cares strictly about my vagina. Ok?! Can you hear me talking? (Even though I'm typing – smile) Seriously, I would love to say he cared about me, but even though I truly in my heart don't think he would bring harm to me intentionally with evil intent, he doesn't love me with the love of God. Do you remember what I said in the very beginning of this book about that? A man isn't truly a good man if he is not a man of God walking in His truth and love. So I have to be a woman of my word with that one. I left and that was it. He emailed me again and I didn't respond. When it is over, YOU DON'T OWE THEM NOTHING!

That same week, no kidding, I was in church on Sunday. My Pastor was getting ready to start his sermon. Now, this is the quietest time in church because all eyes are on him and everyone is fully attentive. He stopped talking and said, "I just have to be obedient to the spirit. Vawn Gretta stands up. Saint the enemy wants to pull you off course and you have to be careful not to fall. There is going to be a man trying to come to specifically defile you and pull you off course to destroy the anointing on your life and you need to stay away from that. He is a true counterfeit. So hold on woman of God and stay in your walk." I ran all over that church because my Pastor hears and he prays for me. He was all in my house and knew what was in my cabinets too! All I can say is thank God I ran out of there. Catch this; I should have NEVER been in there in the first place. I asked God right then to give me the strength to not even go in the places that can harm my walk with Christ. God said, "Then don't give those men access to you." Hello!

Well, this man at my job caused me to dig into the word like never before. I studied not to just memorize and learn but to rightly divide the word. So God was really good with that. To sum this up, I found out that Jehovah Witnesses do not allow the spirit of prophecy and other gifts of the spirit to go forth. Now the one unforgivable sin is the blasphemy of the Holy Spirit. (Matthew 12:31-32) The Holy Spirit empowers these gifts to go forth. You may want to talk to your pastor for further clarity on that. I will say that is was the deciding factor in my deciding not to become Jehovah Witness. We remained good friends and he ended up moving to another state. I asked God to take care of him and God was faithful. One day God showed me that I was going to celebrate his birthday and he had a girlfriend. I woke up and decided to call and check on him because I know that he doesn't celebrate birthdays.

When I talked to him he informed me he was getting married! I was so happy I thought I was going to jump through the phone. He sent me the pictures of the wedding and there was a thick brown girl with long hair. I wondered if that could have been me and then I dismissed that thought. First of all, because it wasn't! And secondly, because I know God didn't propose that. God told me if I find myself asking, "God is he the one", I should know he is not! God repeated that to me over and over. I received that to be true.

Dear Sis,

God is so good. I want to clearly say that once you start walking in purity and start handling yourself the right way the devil will still try to throw you off course and trick you. So don't go crazy at the first man that tries to get next to you even if he is a man of God. That doesn't mean he is your man of God. Please don't get your feelings hurt when you find out that this one isn't your husband either. Remember there is no such thing as rejection when you are walking with God. The world's rejection is God's direction and protection.

Please do not give men access so readily into your life. Yes he really may be your man of God. Great! Give God the time you both need to develop the relationship in the healthiest manner. This is for all ages. I don't care how old you are. None of us have more wisdom than God. You cannot out think your creator. For example, they don't need your email address, job number, your mom's number, your best friend's number or cell number. You don't need theirs either. If they want to talk to you tell them what I said. I told them to find me at 485 Maxey

Rd. in Houston, Texas. That is the address to my church. Hello? Smile. And if they kept asking me for my phone number, I gave them the number to the church; again, because that is where they could find me. So if they really had good intentions, they could come get the word and maybe talk to me. After they meet God approval, then you can slowly start letting them in.

I am sure I don't have to tell you that none of them even came to the church except for one. And that one is going to be sleeping next to me tonight and I now bare his last name. How many of you know that I am now smiling. Isn't it about time that I don't end a chapter crying? I have to take a praise break.

Even a man of God is a HUGE handful. I am so serious. You get into a relationship that is all about God and the devil gets completely pissed off. Satan will work overtime to kill what God created. You, me – we have to have a man that hears from God and prays or honey we are doomed. When you are sick and tired of being sick and tired, God will be waiting. He will empower you and no longer will you risk the 'okky doke' man to come and invade your life by pumping his demonic seed into your precious life barring vessel. Access DENIED! BAAM!

2 Corinthians 3:17-18 King James Version

Now the Lord is that Spirit and where the Spirit of the Lord is, there is liberty. But we all, with open face beholding as in a glass the glory of the Lord, are changed into the same image from glory to glory, even as by the Spirit of the Lord.

Chapter 20 – Embracing the Change

It was now November of 2007 and I was still on the job dealing with an increasingly insecure boss as far as the anointing on my life because I talked too much. I just didn't know how to shut up. You cannot tell everyone your dreams and visions. What I didn't tell her is that I was planning to go back to school to go for my Bachelors in Vocal Music. She had deceivingly passed me over for a very deserving promotion and for that reason God checked her good and hired someone that she didn't expect. And it brought her much discomfort. At this time a customer came IN big and black. Just like I like them.

He saw me and all but fell in love with my beauty. By now that did nothing for me so he was smart enough not to make a big deal out of it. But I thought he was respectful and we began to communicate on the phone. He took me to lunch and I really liked that because that had never happened to me. I was beginning to start attracting men that had quality.

Now at this time, I had finished writing my second play and I had submitted it to my Pastor to read and check so that I could do this one in order and excellence. Well, this man was not a man of God. He was afraid to die and I learned all of this on our lunch date. I began to ask God would he change and should I show him some attention. Then with my heart is said, "Is he the one?" I already knew he would not be my husband. So I just stayed sweet and allowed him to be my friend. I would not let him kiss me either and really he backed off of trying because he knew who I was. One day, on a truly beautiful cool and sunny fall day, he called and invited me to the park near my mother's house. He did that because I had the kids with me and he knows I don't do the 'meet my kids' thing. No way. I really would like to encourage you to not drag your kids along on the roller coaster ride of "I hope he the one LAWD pllleeeaaaasssseeee!" Please do not do that. You are subjecting them to unnecessary disappointment. You and I both know they will encounter enough of that just living life. Protect them from you. Trust me, God gave you everything you need to raise your babies. Trust God.

When we got to the park he sat down and we talked as if we met at the park while the kids played. He explained to me that the girlfriend that he had recently broken up with and he had a deep conversation. He explained to me that she was always trying to get him into church. I told him he should really consider because obviously she loves him a great deal. He did agree and that was the purpose for his visit. He explained that sense he met me, he realized how special his girlfriend was and he wanted to give it a try. He wanted to try and make it work. A part of me was disappointed that my husband still had not found me. But a bigger part of me was pleased because God once again ordered my steps and protected and directed me.

I walked back home with the kids feeling disappointed honestly. But I was not without hope. As I walked I told God that I trusted him. That week I finished reading this one book that was challenging me in all directions. In the book the author said that we should ask God if it is His will that we be married. Her point was to say that if we have to have a mate when God hasn't purposed and ordained such is out of order. It's like saying that just living a life with Jesus isn't' enough. She suggested that we pray and ask God to show us what His purpose is for us in this area. I cried so hard I couldn't see. But I wanted to be free. If I was not supposed to be married I wanted to know quickly so that I can begin to receive freedom from that desire. I cannot put into words just how hard that was. I had to go to God and say that if I am not supposed to be married please show me and give me a heart to receive that and an anointing to walk in it. After seven days I stopped crying about it. Seven is the number of completion and eight is the number of new beginnings and that is just what happened.

In the forward, I mention a ministry, Women Reaching Women. Momma Gwen or Minister Gwen Hart spoke a word in me that was very pivotal. One weekend we were gathered at a sister's in the Lord's house for fellowship. This was December 14th of 2007. We began to pray in the spirit and worship. The word that came forth in prophecy to me was to 'loose the check spirit I have on me.' This is important because the man that God has for me needs to stay away from a controlling spirit. Now God hardly ever spoke to me concerning men so I took that word completely seriously.

Because I worked around all men, I would try this out. Basically, the word was saying I check people too quickly and it is controlling. It was so hard. I had this one customer me to say, now these are truck drivers, "Say honey do I need to fill out this paperwork?" I wanted to say, "Well duh, that is why it is called a customer drop off from you idiot? Hello!" But I didn't I just said, "Yes you do."

Then I would say something as simple as good morning and help yourself to some donuts. One time one of them asked me if there were chocolate donuts in the box. I said no. That turkey said, "Well there will be if you jump in there and then I'll be happy." I guess I don't have to tell you how I had to bite my tongue. But my favorite, while I was trying to lose the 'check spirit' was "Say you need to tell me what this is saying!"

He was talking about a very basic sign in form. I tried to explain it then he said, "Well why don't you just fill it out for me then." I said, "I am so sure you can do it for yourself if you try but I will be right here to help." I was trying to be nice and this one was testing me. So I was about to walk away to my desk when he said the mother of all comments after all of that. "You must need a man." Girl!!!!!! Jesus. My boss, knowing the word that was spoken over me, was in her office at her desk smiling and holding back extreme laughter. See at this job we had to have tough skin to deal with men and we were the only ladies, even with our co-workers, we could say just about anything to the customers. These men were a mess so we had to hold our own. I looked at that man with a forced smile on my face and took a deep breath and I said, "My man is Jesus and I am so happy with him. Of course, you being such a handsome man of God would truly understand that. As a matter of fact, I bet you already knew my man was Jesus and I bet that is why you said that huh? Because I know you are smart. I can tell the way you are so nicely are filling out that form. I will be at my desk to finish helping you when you finish."

When I turned around I was facing my boss and she just looked at me and put her head down to keep from falling out in laughter on the floor. I really did like her even with her faults. I still think she is the best boss I have ever had. Anyway, I passed the test. I wanted to tell that dude, "Look, partner, if you can't figure this out, something serious may be wrong with you; perhaps you can go to the community college and bring back and application for your GED. I can help you fill that out. Or better yet, let me go shopping with you so I can help you spell toothpaste for those cigarette stained cheese looking teeth you have. Looking like a dull set of grills. (Which are supposed to be made in gold) No! Perhaps I should just stab my ears with a knife so that I don't have to go through the pain of listening to your conversation." Then slap the taste out of his mouth, laugh at him in his face and then walk away.

The bottom line is God truly did a work in me and now I was ready. I didn't say all of that. Jesus.

Dear Sis,

I know that God was testing me to see if I could really walk in a way that was not controlling. I passed that test completely. Thank you Jesus. I know that God was proud of me for not trying to hold on to that other guy and embrace him going back to his girlfriend.

I know that God did lead me into change and I thank God that the Holy Spirit did empower me to receive that change and walk in it. Glory to Jesus. For as you have read, it truly was not easy at all. If I can do it anyone can. Thank you Jesus.

Proverbs 4:7-8 King James Version

Wisdom is the principal thing, therefore get wisdom and with all thy getting get understanding. Exalt her, and she shall promote thee; she shall bring thee to honour, and when thou doest embrace her.

Chapter 21 – The Great Counterfeit

Here is some truth; all that you have read was completed in 2008. I had been so afraid of releasing this information. If you don't know, abused people are seriously afraid of "getting their attacker or monster, as I like to call them, in any "trouble." A very good friend of mine said to me recently, "Did they do anything to protect you?" I couldn't speak, because none of them had done a thing. Oh but they did truly cause me pain. She then said, "Well, why are you protecting them. Move forward in what God has called you to do." So here I sit overcoming exhaustion from grief and heartache as I share the most pivotal part of this book. I pray for courage as I cry and write, for truly this chapter looked a whole lot different in 2008 when this book was first finished. That's how much God loves me. He spared me from extra public humiliation.

I had worked so hard to make sure that I had dealt with all of the tears in my life. I read all the self-help books, served in church, walked in purity and decided I would pray this prayer.

"Lord God I give you the desire I have to be married and ask that you just take away until my husband should find me." Sure enough, I found peace and was totally content. I and Jesus were in love. Still, the desire did burn.

Soon after I found that peace, I received a call from a friend of mine. He explained that he had a friend that he thought I should meet because he wrote poetry and was into plays. Well, my business mind was intrigued so I called the guy up. It didn't take me long to figure out this was a setup for a possible relationship. I need to be clear and say I know my friend's heart was in the right place. Just remember and never take for granted that Satan has your number and he is watching you. He sees the angles around you protecting you and lining up to deliver a blessing. Therefore, he will work overtime to try to "look like" God in your life. Do NOT take that for granted. We must trust ourselves and that little burning thought and stirring in our spirits. Lord have mercy!

I am going to choose to make this story shorter than it is for the sheer purpose of this being the last chapter in this book and I truly want to get to the point; and, quite frankly, it hurts to write. I did meet his friend. During our first conversation, I remember thinking, "Wow this guy seems weak, especially in the spirit. I just couldn't see being his woman." I then felt sorry for him because I truly am a compassionate woman. If you have read this book to this point I will safely gather that you are as well, or you are just nosy. HA! Let's laugh at that.

As a single mother, I had needs and my total prayer was to be with a man who treated me right and made me feel like he truly loves me and to be a father for my children. I want you to remember I said that. As noble and harmless as that desire is, it is so detrimental. Why Vawn Gretta? That's an "all about me" prayer. Please feel my heart. If it's only about you, you will not be able to "see" the real truth. Yeah that's and apple, but if you look closely you will see tiny brown spots and if you don't look inside before you bit, you gonna get food poisoning girl!!! Now you have ingested and it's in your system.

I remember the first time I 'felt' like he was the greatest things walking. He offered to help me buy medicine for my son. The next thing was helping me with the down payment for a venue for one of my plays. He wrote me poetry and gave me music CD's to express his love for me. He went as far proclaiming to my entire church that he had found his rib and his wife. I felt so special. My children asked him they could call him Daddy and he told him yes. You can do what you want, but I truly caution you not to let men around your kids until you know that you know he is the one. Of course I just knew this man was the one. Lord just pray, hard – and listen and do what God is saying.

He was so affectionate and passionate and made me feel like a queen both privately and publicly. He even accepted me having herpes and said that he knew that God would heal me and he would be fine with doing our best to walk in purity before we got married. I didn't see the inside of his apartment until after he asked me to marry him on 08/08/08. That's right. Eight is the number of new beginnings. Again, satan knows how to look like God.

I taught him about numbers being important in the word of God. I began to teach him a lot because I felt sorry for him being divorced twice. Who possibly would leave such a great man? He told me how his second wife was a witch and took him to a witch doctor to work on his libido because he didn't want to make love to her because she was so mean and hateful. I believed him. I believed him telling me about sexual abuse when he was a child. I believed him tell me that his parents abandoned him. I felt so sorry for this poor sensitive man. He was everything. Until a woman called after he asked me to marry him and explained that he was her man and said I couldn't have him. He told me that she threatened to hurt me and my children and that's why he kept talking to her. I remember threatening to leave him and my little children were so hurt and upset. I couldn't stand it and I gave him a chance. That was one way of escape I didn't take. My own pastor told me that was a red flag but we all decided to forgive it and believe him.

Right after that he grew very silent and avoided me for a week and I thought I had done something wrong and started to work to fix it. (Read the story of Rebekah in the bible so you don't end up doing what I did.) He eventually started talking to me again. I overlooked that because I thought it was "my fault" for not believing in my man. In keeping with making this story short, we got married. He was so very adamant about me not working although we constantly had financial problems. I would go through trying to find a job, and I am educated and intelligent, yet the search was difficult. As a result, he would say, "See the Lord doesn't want you to work and neither do I." It took about 6 months into our marriage and my husband stopped speaking to me for a week. This happened after I got really sick and he didn't have medical insurance for us. He felt inadequate because we had to ask for financial help to get me seen by a doctor and medical attention. I remember him apologizing because he didn't believe I was sick. I never understood why he would consider that was a lie. He slept on that couch and that's when it started. After that moment all intimacy stopped. For the entire time we were married we made love less than 100 times. In 6 ½ years, approximately 2,200 days he kissed me intimately less than 20 times and never hugged me tightly. Oh, there were moments when he hugged me. If I brought up the idea of intimacy, he would say, "I'm working trying to pay all these bills, I'm not thinking about sex, I'm tired, I need medicine, I need medical help, You did this, You did that." Basically, he blamed it on me and having to take care of me and my children. I got busy writing a new play and wrote my true life.

It was a success. I continued to try my best to make him happy. I found his father that he had not seen in 22 years! I thought surely then, he will love me. I helped him write and edit a book and thought surely he will love me. I figured if I publicly announced always that he was a wonderful husband, he would love me more and be happy again and we would be happy together. There were moments I cried so hard my face hurt. And then I would put on the mask and go to church or a function and be his wife. He never used my name. He would call me wifey from time to time. Whenever he said my name it was so negative. If I brought up intimacy and why he didn't want to touch me, even if it was as simple as holding my hand, he would stop talking to me for a while. Finally when I would come to him and apologize for pressing him about our love life he would then speak to me again. I became so dependent on his foolishness. He never stopped blaming me for everything wrong with our life so I continued to work.

Graphic moments for women in this situation: I remember this man would fall asleep with his hands on my womanhood offering foreplay. Who in the heaven, no what MAN on this planet is going to fall asleep during this course of action?! Not a man that desires women believe me. He never wanted me to see him naked. He was always very sensitive to that idea. That used to make me feels so ugly and unattractive. I hope to forget one of the last times we came together sexually. I happened to look up while in the process and my face looked in the mirror and I saw his face. He was so disgusted. I see his face squinted up and not from pleasure. . He never opened his eyes. Almost as if he was trying to imagine being somewhere else. I thought, "Am I ugly, I know I'm over weight, Im ok aren't I?" Then he just stopped. Almost as if God relieved me from that torture. It was too much. I was pregnant at the time.

From August 2014 to December 2015 we made love 3 times. One of those times produced a beautiful little baby. My pregnancy was very lonely. He decided to sleep in our extra bedroom. I would ask him to come back to the room and never did. One week I tried to hug him he stiffened and refused me. I felt a deep pain in my stomach and tried again. He stiffened but this time touched me. I would cling to moments when we would laugh as a family, although few, and have a sense of hope. We worked with a marriage counseling team (husband and wife) for four years straight. She would always tell me to "stay in a posture of prayer". I always wondered how that wonderful play I wrote was setting the captives free and I was trapped and bound. Still, I prayed.

When my husband didn't hug me, I grabbed my children and went to spend the night in a hotel. I thought about how he said I was too fat, or I wouldn't work (like didn't I try to find a job then you tell me to stop), or how I just don't understand he ain't thinking about sex. Well, I came home because I didn't want to expose my children to that. The next day I was hospitalized and my doctor told me he would not let me go home. My husband stayed at the hospital and I thought I finally had my man back. Maybe it took a near death experience for him to love me. So accepted that fate. Our baby came very healthy. I went home and my blood pressure went up to 225/120 and I was rushed back to the hospital and the doctors and nurses helped me fight for my life. I thought surely I would die and made peace with God. I decided I have work to do and fought for my life.

When I went home I was in a great depression and didn't know it. Not me, Miss strong, Miss Encourager, Miss Over-comer. Not me. Oh yes me. My son nursed me back to health by preparing meals and my daughter stayed near me when I was too scared to go to the bathroom or take a shower by myself. I was afraid of the outside. Hold on, I need to take a cry break. My husband would hold me when it was time to go to be because I felt like I was going to die if I closed my eyes. Who would take care of my babies? I had already been keeping a journal so I started memorizing scriptures dealing with fear and healing.

Soon I went outside to walk and was so proud of myself then my knees gave out and I could barely walk. My husband went back to work about 3 weeks after I had the baby and I was determined to heal and fight depression. One day I went driving in the evening and rolled down the window and hollered, "Depression YOU HAVE TO GO!!!!!" The next morning, I woke up and that same old horrible creature was gone. I decree and declare he will never come back in Jesus name. If you are struggling with depression, you are not alone. Please reach out and get help.

By now, I would ask my husband to come in the bedroom and I would say, "Can you come please just hold me, I won't try to kiss you or have sex." He would say ok but never came and went back to sleep in the extra room. That was only 5 weeks after I fought for my life. I emailed my pastor about it and she said stop asking him and just start praying. So I did. I talk to my marriage counselor about it and she confirmed. She also encouraged me to start seeking the truth. So I did. I said, "Lord, I'm ready for the truth."

One day I was laying in the bed watching an episode of Scandal and it told the story of a gay man being married to a woman at first and then choosing a man. I saw his pain and saw the woman's pain. I felt an elephant size knot well up in my stomach as I watched. I remember the Lord clearly saying to me, "What kind of man doesn't want to touch his wife?" I said, "A cheater." Then I thought about that answer, shoot even a cheater will sleep with his wife. I know that from watching my father. Then I crashed when I looked back at my computer screen with the show on it. It all made sense.

When my husband came home and walked into the room, I asked him to close the door. This is exactly how the conversation went:

"Hey honey I know what is going on with you. I know that you have a struggle with homosexuality." And right there, he literally sunk down to the floor and began to cry. I told him I love him and I can help him if he wants to get delivered. I did really love him.

He said, "Look you can date other men if you want, and we can still be married."

I began to cry, "I don't want that in my life. I want you. How long has this been your struggle?"

He said, "Gay men don't have babies."

My response was, "really? It's that real isn't it?" And he just sat there and teared up and so did I. My stitches from my C-section had not healed yet.

I figured I would work to help him get passed this, after all, I am the suitable help meet. He stopped talking to me for about a week and then I just acted like it didn't happen. I decided to get back in school because I finally realized all of the emotional and verbal abuse I suffered in the marriage had nothing to do with me. He grew cold again and very angry that I got back in school. I didn't want to go back to being a single mother with no way to take care of my babies again.

We ended up losing our home due to mold but had no money to move anywhere else. Ultimately, my dear, awesome mother allowed us to move in. Even there, he slept on her sofa and not in the bed with me. I kept praying for him. From September to November my husband didn't talk to me. Not one word. Expect to tell me about a bill or searching for an apartment. It was so hard to go to school every day knowing my children would be fatherless again and here I am living with my mom as a grown woman; and, my brother lived there. Jesus!! I was surrounded by the reminder of abuse. The walls didn't close in because I had school. He grew colder and meaner towards me but I was encouraged one day by my pastor. She said, "Vawn Gretta I promise you God is going to deliver you. Your husband will either change or God will remove you from the situation. Just stand in righteousness and hold on." I did just that.

I ended up gaining a scholarship to pay for school! I made the Honor's, Dean's and President's list. I made a new young friends that never made me feel old. God sent me an angel to love my voice back to life, Jolie Rocke Brown. Still, the pain of what I thought was a dream come true, turning into a nightmare was very present in my life. Sigh. On Christmas Eve we went to pick up Christmas gifts from the children's Godparents who were also our marriage counselors. The male counselor began to speak about secrets in marriages and how they will keep a marriage from working. He was so loving in the way he ministered it. We left and went home. That evening, my husband came to me and said, "Well I told the truth about my situation and just got it out." I was so happy! I thought, "Wow Imma get my man back!"

I got nosey and looked at his phone and read the text message where he admitted to having 'gay tendencies.' I don't know why that hurt me. I guess reality was too much. Still, I said well if he wants help then I'm still all in. Sadly he never sought help or deliverance and I filed for divorce. He would say he wanted to stay married and I would ask about his "issue" and he would avoid the conversation. I would ask how we could possibly stay married in an ungodly situation. I desperately wanted to help him but I had learned you can't help someone that doesn't want to help. So I prayed this prayer, "Lord if this man means me and my children no good and doesn't want to change, please make it impossible for him to trick me, my family, friends, and pastors any longer." After that, he didn't fight the divorce process. I could see peace in his eyes. He was tired too, poor dear. Yes I could call him all kind of explicit names but in my healing process I have learned, that does no good at all. My Lord. I told him about the divorce date and told him if he wants to come he can but doesn't have to. I was hoping he would come fight for me. I was hoping he would call our marriage counselors or someone and say I want my marriage AND act on it. His words were one thing and his actions were "goodbye." So that's it. Almost 7 years of trying and in 5 minutes the judge said, "You have your name back," and banged his gavel. I left that courthouse dragging my feet. I have no idea why people celebrate divorce.

Dear my beautiful sisters,

Remember when I talked about "all about me" prayers and desires? I want you to think about this the next time you get into a relationship and as you are praying for your mate. If you take out of the equation all that he makes you "feel", what are you left with? And please pay attention to the red flags. I even broke my toe the night before I got married and walked down the aisle with a can. Jesus. God even tried to stop me physically when the woman that he was cheating on me with didn't work. I thought it was an attempt from the devil to destroy what "God" was doing and my marriage counselors at the time, agreed. 1. Listen to your nucleus. 2. Be careful about who you choose to be marriage counselors. Be VERY careful. It took him one month after the divorce was final to begin to ruse another woman in his life to cover his undercover lifestyle. I prayed for her, thankfully it didn't last. What's my point in saying that? Some people really don't change. Move forward, in a forward progressive motion.

I want you to know that your wholeness comes from God. My children have had to recover from the rejection of losing yet another father because he eventually didn't want to deal with them and they could feel it. He cares for the daughter I gave him however. As I finish this book that I wrote 8 years ago, again, I am currently in the healing process of this journey. I am seeing a therapist to make sure I clean myself from the abuse I have suffered in my life as to not repeat the pattern because this hurts and I would not have you go through this.

Being with a man of God isn't enough. The Lord must always be your first and you must fearlessly listen to His reason and instruction even when your flesh doesn't like it. I plead with you to hear me. I beg of you. He would have no other God before him. People always ask me how I didn't *know* that he was struggling. Well I took the pure walk seriously. Yes there were times we got way to close and I thought, "Yaay we will have fun enjoying each other because this is hard to stay apart." But alas, I didn't really know his sexual habits. Please sisters don't choose to *learn* a man's sexual habits so you don't end up like me. I really don't know what to tell you in order to avoid that. Just really be close to God and choose to listen to him. Look at the man's fruit of his life and be sensitive to the Holy Spirit. I suppose I have a few more books to write for explanation. ☺

Don't be afraid of loneliness. You are never alone for we all have a comforter. "Yeah Vawn Gretta but girl I need someone to hold me at night." You better not let that rule you Sis. Hear the voice of the Lord. Whether you have suffered physical, mental, emotional or verbal abuse, the scar is the same Sis.

Now let me encourage you to seek help. Be wise and get to a safe place especially if you have children. You are valuable and God loves you – I love you. You deserve the best, so fearlessly love yourself.

Remember when I said at the beginning of this chapter, "still, the desire did burn?" Some men and women of God would say that one should lay a desire down and not think about it, especially when it comes to being married. I say, no – I scream, the bible says that we should be a prisoner of hope and God would restore twice as much unto us. (Zechariah 9:12) I do believe that it is very critical that we be not in bondage to anything and that we be not brought under the power of anything. Yet, we should not abandon that which God has placed in us to believe. Now we have to be very careful here. Let me try to explain this the very best I way I am able. I am a musician. I love music. If I didn't have music in my life I would truly perish. I can't breathe without it because truly it is my calling. Being on stage performing musically and theatrically is my desire right in line with my calling and I know that God uses it to bring people beauty for their ashes. If you were a minister you would say, "That's awesome sister! Walk in that!" Conversely, if I say I know that I am called to be a family woman and wife; and, I know I am a wonderful wife, it has always been a desire right in line with my musical purposes - what would a minister say to me? I know God says, be a prisoner of hope. I know that God says seek Him first and He will give me the desires of my heart. I know God says hope deferred makes the heart sick but when the desire comes it is a tree of life.

Therefore, I say to you believe what God is saying to you. If you have earnestly sought the Lord and He has spoken to you undoubtedly, walk in your hope for marriage. However don't let it rule you or place you in bondage. I refuse to pretend that I have that down to a science. I would be lying. I will say that, that desire does not cause me to be in despair, anguish or in a state of self-pity. I will honestly tell you that loneliness is a booger! Oh my goodness! Especially after you have longed for so long and been starved of love and companionship that should have been yours. Sigh. Be courageous and do not let loneliness rule you and control your decisions. That's trouble. Lay the desire on the altar, find a wise mentor(s), thank God for your gifts and do you best to wait patiently on him.

Stay focused on you. You are no good to yourself or anyone if you live like a worthless victim. Remember failure is an event, not a person. You are so much more than the hurt you have lived through and so am I my dear sister(s).

Never forget that there is a Nucleus, and inner you that lives and will never die! I don't care how lost you feel, how empty, how anything, know that you are alive and well and nothing can harm that part of you. Because only God and you have access to it and nothing and no one can destroy, YOU!

Please write yourself a simple personal declaration that you can say to yourself every day. Please. You must fill your head with thoughts of beauty and loveliness toward yourself to drown out the destructing words floating around in your psyche.

Lord God I pray that the captives have been set free. I pray that you have brought beauty for our ashes and that the root that allows abuse will be uprooted and never again planted in Jesus name. I pray for the courage to get away from the source of abuse, even if self-inflicted now. Truly we trust you and know you love us. In Jesus name. Amen

Philippians 4: 4-13 KJV

Rejoice in the Lord always: and again I say, Rejoice. Let your moderation be known unto all men. The Lord is at hand. Be careful for nothing; but in everything by prayer and supplication with thanksgiving let your requests be made known unto God. And the peace of God, which passeth all understanding, shall keep your hearts and minds through Christ Jesus. Finally, brethren, whatsoever things are true, whatsoever things are honest, whatsoever things are just, whatsoever things are pure, whatsoever things are lovely, whatsoever things are of good report; if there be any virtue, and if there be any praise, think on these things. Those things, which ye have both learned, and received, and heard, and seen in me, do: and the God of peace shall be with you. But I rejoiced in the Lord greatly, that now at the last your care of me hath flourished again; wherein ye were also careful, but ye lacked opportunity. Not that I speak in respect of want: for I have learned, in whatsoever state I am, therewith to be content. I know both how to be abased, and I know how to abound: everywhere and in all things I am instructed both to be full and to be hungry, both to abound and to suffer need. I can do all things through Christ which strengtheneth me.

One last encouragement. I would like to invite you to receive a free gift. This is a gift of love and everlasting life. Meaning, if you were to die today you would spend eternity with God the Father in the most wonderful bliss and beauty. Also, to live a life wrapped in the comfort of knowing that somehow, someway the most powerful being has you personally in mind every second of everyday. How? So very easy. Please read the following prayer:

"Lord, I do not know much about you but I realize I am a sinner because I have not confessed that Jesus is Lord. So today I ask you to come into my heart and guide me. I confess that Jesus Christ, your son, died on the cross to save me from my sins so that I may have everlasting life with you, Lord. Help me, Lord, as I lean on you for understanding, wisdom, and support so that I may live an abundant life with you. Thank you for loving me first and bringing me to you. In Jesus Christ name I pray, Amen."

Now give yourself the biggest hug! Love you to life and God bless you real big!

Epilogue

I want you to know I did graduate with honors with my Bachelors of Arts degree in Vocal Music Performance from Texas Southern University and I am now a Graduate student at the University of Saint Thomas! There I am pursuing a Sacred Music degree. We left with just our clothes from that situation and Harvey took even the clothes we had! BUT GOD! God continues to open doors. I am a Music Appreciation teacher and Choir Director at a high school as well! My children have overcome hurt and pain with counseling. We are all functional and doing very well. I have a super village of support and truly feel loved. Mostly I work daily to continue to love myself and be patient in my wait for my desire. I will have this story in another book coming soon. I stay focused on me and the walk God has called me to walk. Love you BIG.

Remember, "YOU TOO, CAN ACHIEVE!!!!"

Resources for you to consider:

1. The Bible.
2. *"Changer Your Mind and Your Life Will Follow"* by Karen Casey
3. *"Knight in Shining Armor"* by P.B. Wilson
4. *"Adult Children of Alcoholics"* by Janet Woititz
5. *"The Three Battlegrounds"* by Francis Frangipane

About the Author

Vawn Gretta is a Vocalist (Classical, Jazz, Soul and Gospel), Actress, Songwriter, Director, Author, Vocal and Performance Coach and Playwright, Vawn Gretta Stearnes was born to share love through the gifting of creative arts. She began her musical career singing, playing the piano and flute at a very early age.

Vawn Gretta graduated with an Associate of Arts Degree in Vocal Music Performance in the spring of 2007 and a Bachelor of Arts Degree in Vocal Music Performance Degree from Texas Southern University, with honors in spring 2017. She is currently pursuing a Masters in Sacred Music (Vocal concentration) at the University of Saint Thomas in Houston.

In 2005, Vawn Gretta was produced her first musical, "Opening Night", in 2008 "The Prodigals in He's Got to be Real" and in 2013 to present "Ramon and Gretta"; and, all shows Vawn Gretta wrote, produced, directed, acted and wrote the music in the plays. In 2013, Vawn Gretta released her first solo project, "His Love." She the author of two books, "30 Days to a Better Woman" and "Dear Sis".

Vawn Gretta is the Mistress of Ceremonies for "Notes and Rhythms" (an elegant night of jazz and poetry) and many other events from informal to black tie events. She is also the founder of Visions and Dreams, which supports single parents pursuing education and enhancing creative and fine arts in the lives of their children.

Striving for the very best through the arts will always be Vawn Gretta's passion and she will continue to do so in elegance and excellence.